A LOSS OF ROSES

a
loss
of
roses

A new play by

William Inge

With a foreword by the author

Random House, New York

With deep affection for

AUDREY WOOD,

*who stands staunchly by
until theatrical blood
turns into catsup*

FOREWORD

After preparing a play for a New York opening, particularly if the play fails, it is very comforting for the author to get the manuscript back into his own hands and start getting it ready for his publisher. Then the author owns his script again, and he can clear from his mind all the confusing experiences he has had to cope with during production: the demands for cuts, the rearrangements of scenes to fit the scenic design, the changing emphases upon character. In the midst of all these demands, it is very difficult for an author to remember the play he wrote, to hold onto the essential parts without which the play's meaning cannot be expected to be clear. Once in charge of his own script again, the author has a feeling "Now I can make my play what I really want it."

This play is not the play that was produced in New York last November. The manuscript with which we started production was published in the January, 1959, issue of *Esquire* magazine, but it was greatly changed by the time the play opened at the Eugene O'Neill Theatre. Now I can't remember why all the changes were thought necessary at the time, but working under the pressure that exists in the theatre today, people become excited and mistrust their best instincts. During production time, I was forced to do a great deal of writing on the characters of Helen and Kenny, making their relationship clearer. Some of this writing was made necessary because so much material had been cut from the first half of the play that I had to make explicit many dramatic values that I had intended to be merely implied. Yet, some of these rewrites were good, and I have incorporated the good ones into this edition.

The production of *A Loss of Roses* was a complete failure. And yet, I have never gone into production with a play in which I had such complete confidence. Perhaps I was too confident of the play, for I could never really believe that it would not succeed until the last few days of our out-of-town engagement, when suddenly I realized that the play I had thought I had written was not happening on the stage. By that time, it was too late to make all the changes that would have been necessary. I tried to prevent its coming into New York but this would have brought me a greater personal financial loss than I could have handled. I have never felt so trapped. Finally, there seemed nothing to do but let the show come in, knowing that it would meet with failure, knowing that it could have been very successful. It was most disheartening.

I believe now that the most serious mistake I made was to permit the New York production to end with the parting scene between the mother and son, Helen and Kenny. As first conceived, the play ended rightly with the departure of Lila, and thus the ending should have remained. For it is really Lila's play, and to refuse her the ending brought about a change in the emphasis on character that confused all the other values of the play. I am only sorry that I could not see this until it was too late. But in this edition, I have been able to right the wrong that was done to this already mistreated character.

I feel that *A Loss of Roses* is a timely play. To be sure, it deals only with individuals, not representing any class or race struggle, not living with any consciousness of the atom bomb or of rockets to outer space. But it deals with individuals who, like people today seeking an inner peace in the midst of terrifying social change, must come to deal with evil in their lives, either to be destroyed or to find themselves strengthened. And I purposely set the play in the Depression because I feel that underneath our inflated prosperity today, there is a serious depression which we are struggling not to face. I feel that in *A Loss of Roses*, I have been able to make clearer than in any of my other plays an existentialist view I have come to adopt during the last ten years, that man can only hope for an individual peace in the world; and like Whitman, "I swear nothing is good to me now that ignores individuals." All attempts to deal with men in groups, or as objects of time and environment, I think, fail.

WILLIAM INGE

New York City
January, 1960

A Loss of Roses *was first presented by Saint Subber and Lester Osterman at the Eugene O'Neill Theatre, New York City, November 28, 1959, with the following cast:*

(In order of appearance)

Mrs. Helen Baird (A woman in her forties)	Betty Field
Kenny (Her son, a young man of twenty-one)	Warren Beatty
Geoffrey Beamis (Jelly) (A neighborhood friend of Kenny)	Michael J. Pollard
Lila Green (A small-time tent-show actress in her early thirties)	Carol Haney
Ronny Cavendish (An aging juvenile actor)	James O'Rear
Mme. Olga St. Valentine (A tent-show actress, about fifty)	Margaret Braidwood
Ricky Powers (A tent-show actor, about Lila's age)	Robert Webber
Mrs. Mulvaney (A young mother)	Joan Morgan

Directed by Daniel Mann

Setting by Boris Aronson

Costumes by Lucinda Ballard

Lighting by Abe Feder

Music edited by Robert Emmett Dolan

The action of the play takes place in the modest bungalow of Mrs. Helen Baird in a small town outside of Kansas City. It is 1933.

Act One

Scene 1. Late summer.

Scene 2. Two hours later.

Scene 3. Late the next morning.

Act One ~~One~~ *TWO*

Scene 1. One month later.

Scene 2. Early the next morning.

Act One

A mother and her son sit at a table in the kitchen of their modest little bungalow, eating their supper. The time is 1933, in late summer. The mother is MRS. HELEN BAIRD, *a woman in her middle forties who works during the day as a nurse in the hospital of the little Kansas town they live in, close to Kansas City. She is a tired-looking woman who long ago gave up her youth and no longer strives to make herself sexually attractive. There is still a little beauty, however, in the simple dignity of her sad face, a face that has looked on tragedy and never forgotten it.*

The son, KENNETH—*or* KENNY—*is a young man, or boy, of twenty-one. He works as a filling-station attendant in the town and is now dressed in the soiled uniform of his job, a pair of greasy coveralls. He is a nice-looking boy who wears a mysterious look of misgiving on his face, as though he bears some secret resentment that he has never divulged, that he has perhaps never admitted to his consciousness.*

The house itself, small and poor, still retains a little of the dignity that HELEN *shows in her face, and there are a few pieces of furniture in the various rooms that bring a little style and richness from an earlier day. The house suggests that the people in it once saw better times.*

Next door to the BAIRDS' *little bungalow is a vacant lot where, during the summer, a variety of attractions appears. At present a roller-skating rink has moved in to attract the summer trade. A little later in the scene, the music from the rink will be heard, a kind of calliope playing monotonous, swinging waltzes.*

3

At their supper, HELEN *and* KENNY *eat in a rather businesslike way, as though a meal were something to be gotten out of the way, like housecleaning or laundry.* KENNY *is in one of his frequent bad moods, indulging in the kind of stubborn, bad nature that young people often express in resistance to their elders.*

KENNY All right. How long's she gonna stay?

HELEN I don't know, Kenny.

KENNY She may just stay on forever, and I'll have to spend the rest of my life, sleeping on the davenport, dressing behind the screen, while she takes over my room. *My* room.

HELEN You're exaggerating this.

KENNY I bet I have to spend the whole summer sleeping on the davenport.

HELEN She won't be here that long.

KENNY How do you know? What'd she say when she called you? And what'd *you* say?

HELEN She called from Pennant Junction just before you got home from the filling station. She said the show had closed, and that she had no money and no place to go. She asked if she could work for us again, and do the housework and the cooking. Of course I said yes.

KENNY How do ya think I feel, coming home from work this evening, and finding I'd been moved outa my room. *My* room! And all my clothes moved into the living-room closet, and the davenport turned into a bed for me.

4

HELEN (*Truly concerned with his feelings*) Oh, I'm sorry, Kenny.

KENNY God damn!

HELEN (*Her ire raised*) Kenny, I'm sorry but I still won't allow you to swear like that in my house. No. I won't permit it.

KENNY *Your* house? *Your* house? I pay half on everything now, don't I? Don't forget that. I turn over half my salary to you every week, don't I? That makes this just as much my house as yours.

HELEN (*Humbled*) I apologize.

KENNY (*Mocking*) "*My* house! *My* house!" That's a woman for ya.

HELEN Don't you think it's right that you should pay half, now that you're out of high school and working?

KENNY I didn't say it wasn't right.

HELEN You act so begrudging about it. I work hard, too, re-member, and I bring home half my salary, which isn't any more than yours.

KENNY Who said I was begrudging?

HELEN No one said it. You act it.

KENNY I wouldn't be begrudging, maybe, if I had the rights around here I deserve.

HELEN Kenny, it offends me to hear you take the Lord's name in vain. Can't you understand that? It *offends* me.

KENNY   I get used to cussing like that at the station.

HELEN   I wish you would stop. It doesn't become you. It doesn't become anyone. But in my presence, I insist that you not use such language. You've got to pay me that respect as your mother.

KENNY (*Wanting to be rid of the subject*)   OK. OK.

HELEN   Now I'm sorry you're having to give up your room. I'm very sorry. But I've got to help Lila in any way I can. But inasmuch as I asked her here, I'm willing to give up *my* room and sleep on the davenport. So after I straighten up here in the kitchen, we'll move your things back and . . .

KENNY   Oh sure! That makes me feel fine, doesn't it? Letting my mother make a big sacrifice like that.

HELEN   I wouldn't look on it as a sacrifice. I'll do it gladly.

KENNY   Forget it.

HELEN   I'm serious. I'll do it gladly.

KENNY   Forget it. The only thing that makes me sore is ya din even *ask* me. No. This old dame calls you up on the phone and asks can she come here to camp awhile, and you say, Sure, we'll just toss old Kenny out and give you *his* room, without even asking me.

HELEN (*Truly repentant, seeing now her casual mistake*)   Oh, Kenny, that was wrong of me. Please forgive me.

KENNY   If I'm gonna pay half on things here in my own home, I'm gonna insist on my rights, too.

HELEN   Of course, of course. Oh, that was rude of me. I should have called you at the station and asked you. But try to forgive me, Son. It's still hard for me to realize that you're out of high school now, and working, and . . . and are no longer my little boy.

   (*She pats him fondly on the head and he is placated*)

KENNY   OK, then. Let's forget it. I'll sleep on the davenport.

HELEN   Here's what we'll do. When your Aunt Lila comes, I'll tell her that we can let her have your room for one week, and that if she stays longer, then *she'll* have to sleep on the davenport.

KENNY (*Happy now*)   OK.

HELEN   Does that make you feel better?

KENNY   It's OK. Am I supposed to call her *Aunt?*

HELEN   Well, you can do as you like about that. She's not your real aunt. You only called her that when you were a little boy down in Oklahoma. She's no blood relation.

KENNY   It's all I can do to remember her.

HELEN   Oh, you were just crazy about her when you were a little boy. You loved your Aunt Lila then. It used to make me feel a little jealous.

KENNY   Now she's an actress?

HELEN   Yes. She left town with a show, when you were only five or six.

KENNY   Before Dad died?

HELEN   Yes. Several years before.

KENNY   Gee, I never knew an actress before.

HELEN   Neither did I. But we're going to have one in our house. Oh, you'll come to like Lila again. I'm sure you will. She was a very sweet girl when I knew her, big-hearted and . . . and beautiful, too. Oh, Lila Green was the most beautiful girl in town.

KENNY   Was she a servant for us?

HELEN   Well, in a way, but she was part of the family, too. After you were born, I paid her a little money to help me with the housework and to look after you. That was when your father was alive and we had a little more money. She was just a girl then, younger than you are now, and going to school. Her family lived next door to us. Remember?

KENNY   A little.

HELEN   They were very poor, and her parents fought. It was a stepfather she had, and a stepbrother older than she. It wasn't a very happy life for her. I advised her to go with a tent show when she had the chance. One of the men in the show, one of the two brothers who ran the show, fell in love with her and wanted to marry her. She always had a little talent at singing and acting, and she was thrilled by the offer, so I advised her to go. I didn't know much about the show or the people in it, but I felt that any life would be better than the life she had at home. I had a letter from her a few months after she'd gone. I don't know how she found out we had

8

moved back here to Kansas, after your father died. Maybe her mother wrote her.

KENNY Did you say she was *driving* here from Pennant Junction?

HELEN That's what she said.

KENNY (*With new interest*) That means she's got a *car*.

HELEN But I don't know if it's hers or not. She said she was with some other people. The show closed someplace up in Nebraska. They're all on their way to Kansas City.

KENNY I wouldn't mind her being here if she had a car.

HELEN If she does have one, does that necessarily mean she'd let you use it?

KENNY Maybe.

HELEN If you want a car so much, you should have taken that job in the airplane factory over in Wichita. A splendid job like that in times like these, and you act as though you had such offers every day.

KENNY I've got a good job here, don't I?

HELEN This little town doesn't offer any future for a young man. You know that, Kenny. You just don't want to admit it. (*There is a brief silence as she looks at him, waiting for a response that doesn't come*) You just don't want to leave home, do you?

9

KENNY I just don't see what's so wonderful about going to Wichita and working in an airplane factory.

HELEN You're twenty-one years old now. You've been out of high school two years. You have ability and you've had chances to get away and improve yourself, but you turn them all down. What's wrong with you, Kenny? What's holding you?

KENNY I'm just taking my time, that's all. I'm not worried about the future. I'm just not gonna rush into things. (*Changes the subject quickly*) Mom, there's a swell car I can get for three hundred bucks, fifty down payment.

HELEN I just can't get you to be serious about things, can I?

KENNY Listen, Mom, it's a Chevy coupe, only three years old. I know it's in good condition cause I've worked on it at the station. Used to belong to Al Ward before he lost his job. If you could handle the down payment, only fifty bucks, I can handle the rest of it in the fall. (*Becomes more affectionate now*) Think of it, Mom. I could take you riding and take you to the movies in it.

HELEN You make as much money as I do and it's you who want the car.

KENNY I just don't happen to have the money right now, but I can pay you back in the fall. How about it, Mom?

HELEN No. This country is in a serious Depression now, and we should be thankful for the things we do have: a roof over our heads, good jobs, plenty of food and clothing, and no fear of being cold in the winter. I don't think it becomes us to complain about not having a car.

KENNY It doesn't do any harm to wish for things, does it?

HELEN Sometimes it makes us discontent with what we have. Do you want any more of the fried potatoes?

KENNY No.

HELEN (*Getting up from the table*) I'll put the dessert on. I brought home a pie from the baker this evening.

KENNY (*Glancing at the pie on the shelf*) *Looks* good.

HELEN Lemon meringue. You've always liked lemon meringue pie.

KENNY I like it when *you* make it.

HELEN (*Setting a piece of pie before him*) Kenny, I just don't have the time or the energy to come home here after a day's work and make you a pie. And it's foolish for me to go to all that trouble when the Butter Nut Bakery can sell them so cheap. Now, how do you like it?

KENNY (*Having sampled the pie, he shoves it away disdainfully*) It's awful.

HELEN (*Hurt*) Kenny!

KENNY I don't like store food.

HELEN Kenny, I just can't feed you like I used to. Can't you understand that? You keep expecting me to do things and to be something that I simply can't be, any more. And you seem to hold it against me that I don't cook for you any more, that I no longer wash your socks and shirts. That hurts me, Kenny.

KENNY   Ya bring home a lousy pie. So what!

HELEN   Kenny, I do my best to make a home for you. I do my best.

KENNY   I know you do, Mom.

HELEN   But you still seem to want me to wait on you hand and foot, like you were a baby. You're grown up now, Kenny. You can't expect me to look after you as I did when you were a child.

KENNY   OK. Do you want me to eat the pie just to make you happy?

HELEN   You've got a lot to learn before you get married and settle down with a wife. That's all I've got to say.

KENNY   Who says I'm gonna get married?

HELEN   (*Taken back a little*)   Kenny . . . ! You know you'll want to some day.

KENNY   (*Lighting a cigarette*)   I don't know anything of the kind.

HELEN   Why, Kenny, of course you'll get married some day.

KENNY   There's not a girl in town I'd look at.

HELEN   You're just saying that.

KENNY (*Harshly*)   I mean it.

HELEN   The little Caswell girl down the street, so pretty. And I admire her. Working in her father's law office this year instead of going away to school. She passes the house every morning on her way to work, and if you knew half as much about women as you pretend to at times, you'd know she *walks* instead of driving the car because she *hopes* that you'll walk with her some day.

KENNY (*Slamming his fists*)   I *hate* Miriam Caswell.

HELEN   Why, Kenny? Give me one good reason.

KENNY   I just hate her. That's all.

HELEN   You've got to have a reason for hating somebody.

KENNY   Snobby. Goes around with her nose in the air all the time. Acting so darn superior.

HELEN   She *is* superior. And you can't hold it against her if she acts a little proud. Heaven knows *you're* a proud one. You ought to be willing to allow a girl *her* pride, too.

KENNY (*Laying down the law*)   Just don't talk about Miriam Caswell again.

HELEN   All right. But if you were a little *nicer* to girls, maybe . . . Well, you do appear bad-natured lots of the time, Kenny, and . . . if you expect *nice* girls to like you, you have to go out of your way a little to be thoughtful and courteous.

KENNY I'm gonna be *myself*.

HELEN Is being yourself just being pig-headed and stubborn? Isn't being yourself ever being nice, too?

KENNY I can't be nice unless I mean it.

HELEN (*Knowing she is treading on dangerous ground*) So, the girls who hang out down at the drugstore and over at the skating rink get all your attentions, girls who don't expect anything from a boy but his *physical* attentions.

KENNY (*Sounding off*) I'm twenty-one years old. I don't need you to tell me what kinda girls to see.

HELEN (*Hotly*) Not one of the girls you see means anything to you. No. You don't want to be bothered by a nice girl because *she* would mean a little responsibility to you, wouldn't she?

KENNY (*In a loud voice*) I've heard enough.

HELEN (*Restraining herself*) All right. But I just think you should remember that *love*, like everything else in the world, doesn't mean much unless you earn it and deserve it.

KENNY You're always trying to talk me into getting married. Whatsa matter? What ya rushing me for?

HELEN (*Not having thought of it this way: a little guilty*) Why, Kenny! What makes you say a thing like that?

KENNY Am I a pest around here? Do I bother you just being here? Ya wanta get rid of me?

HELEN   Kenny, don't talk like that. You *know* I don't feel that way.

KENNY   I've always tried to help you since Dad died, haven't I? Since I've been old enough. I do all the things around here that *he'd* do, don't I? Or try to. I mow the lawn and take care a the furnace and burn the trash. What'd you do without me?

HELEN   I'd miss you very much, Kenny.

KENNY   Then why hurry things? I got a good job and I could look after you, Mom. You wouldn't have to work at all, if you din want to . . .

HELEN   Oh, Kenny! I wouldn't *think* of letting you support me.

KENNY   Why not? I'd be glad to. (*He is beginning to soften*) I don't really mean it, Mom, when I put up a big squawk about my share of the expenses. Honest, I'd be glad to look after *every*thing, if you'd stay home and . . . look after things, and . . .

HELEN   . . . and cook better dinners for you?

KENNY   Well, yah! And quit bossing me all the time.
(*Playfully, he puts an arm around her and tries to kiss her, but she withdraws like a shy maiden*)

HELEN   Now, Kenny!

KENNY   What's wrong with showing a little affection?

HELEN   You're too old to still be making love to me like you did when you were a baby.

KENNY   Judas Priest! It doesn't mean anything.

HELEN   I'm your mother, Kenny, and I have to show my love for you now in other ways. You got too used to my affection when you were little, Kenny. After your father died, and you were all I had. It's not the same now, Kenny.

KENNY   Forget it. I'm just trying to be nice to you and tell you I can look after you, and you act like it was something unholy.

HELEN   Kenny, I couldn't let myself be dependent on you.

KENNY   Ya din feel that way when Dad was alive. You din work when *he* was alive. I can look after you just as well as he did.

HELEN   Kenny, you're *not* your father. Maybe I'm *afraid* of needing you. Did you ever stop to think of that? I have to be practical about things. *I* know you'll want to get married some day, and how would your wife feel if you had a mother to support? I've got to be prepared for the day you leave, and I'd feel a lot better seeing you married to some nice, sensible girl than . . . picking up those cheap girls down at the drugstore and . . .

KENNY   A-men!
        (*He stalks away*)

HELEN   Oh, Kenny!

KENNY   I've heard all I want to for tonight.

HELEN   All right, Kenny! All right. (*She begins to clear the table now. In the background, from the vacant lot, come the sounds of the organ playing its raucous waltzes*) Oh, dear! there it goes again. Every summer we have to be pestered by that hurdy-gurdy at the skating rink. I'll be glad when they're gone and the religious revival comes back. I much prefer listening to hymns to that hurdy-gurdy.

KENNY Hallelujah, Brother! We'll all be saved.

HELEN Don't make fun. You may want to feel saved some day, yourself.
    (HELEN *exits into kitchen to wash dishes.* KENNY *wanders to the front porch, dropping to the doorstep. The sun is setting and the atmosphere is still. A neighborhood crony of* KENNY's *whistles from the distance. It is* JELLY BEAMIS. KENNY *looks up; then* JELLY *calls*)

JELLY (*Off*) Hey, Ken! Whatcha doin'?

KENNY Bakin' a cake, lame-brain. What does it look like?
    (JELLY *comes running on*)

JELLY I mean, are ya doin' anything tonight?

KENNY No plans.

JELLY How 'bout lookin' in at the pool hall? Joe Myers'll be there and he's got a lotta home brew in his basement.

KENNY I dunno.

JELLY Then we could come back here and go to the skating rink. There'll be some girls there. How 'bout it, Ken?

KENNY OK. After a while.

JELLY How 'bout a smoke, Ken?

KENNY Is that all ya came over here for, to mooch a cigarette?

JELLY No, Ken, honest. We're buddies, aren't we?

KENNY When are ya gonna buy some, for Pete's sake?

JELLY Geez, I haven't had any money for so long, I've forgotten what it looks like, Ken.

KENNY (*Takes out his pack reluctantly*) Here.

JELLY Thanks, Ken. I'm gonna pay you back some day. You'll see.

KENNY If you ever paid me back, I'd have enough smokes to keep me the resta my life.

JELLY (*Lighting up*) Aw, I haven't bummed that many off ya, Ken.

KENNY I haven't seen you with a pack of cigarettes on ya since the night you graduated from high school.

JELLY I didn't get a job like you did, Ken. I never see any dough at all except when the old lady gives me a little change for delivering the washings. Makes me feel like a crumb. How'd you like to have to depend on the money your old lady made takin' in washings? Besides, I had a pack last Sunday.

KENNY I didn't see any of them.

JELLY   I came over here but you was out.

KENNY   What are ya gonna do for money if we pick up any girls tonight?

JELLY   I'll just say, " 'I can't give you anything but love, baby.' "

KENNY   And she'll say, "I wanta go for a ride in a car," and "I want a double malt with a toasted cheese sandwich," and "I wanta go to the movie."

JELLY   I'll just have to give her an I.O.U., promising to give her all those things after I get a job.

KENNY   Yah? And maybe she'll give *you* an I.O.U. promising to give you what *you* want then, too.

JELLY   Well, how 'bout you? I don't notice *you* spendin' any money on the girls we pick up. You always say, "Sure, baby, we'll go downtown and get a malt pretty soon." Then you get your kicks and find out you lost your dough.

KENNY   I'm not wastin' any money on the bags we pick up.

JELLY   You're tight, Ken.

KENNY   (*In stout defense*)   I am *not*. I'm just as generous as the next fellow, with anyone I like.

JELLY   You never take anyone to the movies but your old lady.

KENNY   I don't put any of the bags we pick up in the same class with my mom.

JELLY Well, my mom's OK, too, but I don't intend to marry her.

KENNY My mom doesn't have a husband to do things for her. I feel sorry for her. I want to do everything for her I can.

JELLY OK. Don't get sore.

KENNY Who says I'm sore?

JELLY Ken, Joe Myers was tellin' me about the things they got goin' on over in Kanz City now. Do you know they got a night club there with naked waitresses?

KENNY No kiddin'?

JELLY Yah! he says Kanz City's the wildest town on the map now. He says you can walk down Twelfth Street and pick up all the girls you want. He brought back a lot a dirty pittures, too. He bought 'em off a redcap at the bus station.

KENNY You crazy guy. That's all you ever think about.

JELLY That's just 'cause I don't *get* as much as you do.

KENNY Who says?

JELLY I know your kind. You're the kind that gets all he wants and never talks about it.

KENNY Well, if you'd quit talkin' so much about it, maybe you'd get some, too.

JELLY But girls like you, Ken. I mean, I do all right sometimes, but they really go for you. You could have any girl you wanted, I bet you could even get to Miriam Caswell.

KENNY   Who wants to?

JELLY   Aw, come off it, Ken. You know she's a good-lookin' girl.

KENNY   Maybe.

JELLY   Even if she is stuck up, you gotta admit she's good-lookin'.

KENNY   She can keep her good looks for all I care.

JELLY   Man. I'd eat dirt for that.

KENNY   I don't eat dirt for anybody.

JELLY   Why is it, girls like her can make a guy feel so crummy?

KENNY   They just wanta prove they're better'n he is. That's all.

JELLY   Ya think so?

KENNY   Sure.

JELLY   I'm allus afraid I'm gonna hurt a girl like that, or get her dirty, or something. Know what I mean?

KENNY   (*Who knows only too well*)   Yah. I know.

JELLY   It takes real guts to make out with a girl like her.

KENNY   I just don't think about girls like her. I just don't think about 'em.

(*He spits through his teeth as though punctuating his statement*)

WOMAN'S VOICE (JELLY'S MOTHER, *calling shrilly from a distance*) Geoffrey! Geoffrey Beamis! I want you home now. You have to run some errands.

JELLY   There she is. I gotta beat it. Wanta go with me to deliver laundries?

KENNY   Can we use your car when we're through to pick up some girls?

JELLY   I'm sorry, Ken. But the old man just can't afford to use the car now, except for Mom's laundry. Besides, it's so old, it's about ready to fall apart.

KENNY   I gotta stay here awhile, anyway. We're having company.

JELLY   Yah? Who?

KENNY   Some woman that took care of me when I was a kid. She's gonna be staying with us awhile. Isn't that a pain?

WOMAN'S VOICE (*More impatient now*)   Geoffrey! You come here this instant.

JELLY (*Running off*)   S'long, Ken. I'll see ya at the pool hall about nine o'clock.

KENNY   OK, Jell, see ya.

> (*It isn't quite dark yet. Enough sunlight remains to make the atmosphere dusky.* KENNY *continues sitting on the doorstep.* HELEN *leaves the kitchen now and comes out to join him*)

HELEN   No sign of Lila yet?

KENNY   Nope.

HELEN   My watch has stopped again. What time have you?

KENNY   Seven-thirty.

HELEN   (*Produces a small leather coin purse from her apron pocket*)   Kenny! (KENNY *looks at her inquiringly*) I found this in one of your pockets when I was sending your uniforms to the laundry.

KENNY   (*Looking at the purse, his face inscrutable*)   Oh!

HELEN   It's a woman's purse, isn't it?

KENNY   (*His eyes evasive, his voice sounding unconcerned*) Yah . . . I guess.

HELEN   Do you know whose?

KENNY   No. I found it at the station. It musta fallen outa somebody's car.

HELEN   Well, take it back to the station and try to find out who it belongs to. Will you?

23

KENNY It's just a purse I found. It's not worth anything. There wasn't any money in it.

HELEN Just the same, Kenny, take it back. Take it back.

KENNY OK.
> (KENNY *takes the purse, holding it in his hand, rubbing it between his fingers.* HELEN *now tries to make her voice sound normal, as though the incident were forgotten*)

HELEN Was that Jelly Beamis here you were talking to?

KENNY Yah.

HELEN Poor Mrs. Beamis, having to take in laundry, while that lazy husband of hers sits around and does nothing.

KENNY He can't get a job. There's a Depression, haven't you heard? Millions of men can't get jobs.

HELEN Mr. Beamis was out of a job long before the Depression. I've decided that work and Mr. Beamis just don't get along with each other. She's been earning the living ever since we moved here. Is Jelly a nice boy?

KENNY (*In an affected voice*) Simply a lovely boy! Dear, dear! I never knew of such an angelic character.

HELEN I asked you a civil question.

KENNY Jelly's OK.
> (*A car is heard off left*)

HELEN Oh, here she is! Oh, I can't wait to see her. (*Starting off left, she stops a moment and looks at* KENNY) You'll . . . take that back, won't you, Kenny?

KENNY I'm telling you it's just something I found at the station.

HELEN Just the same, take it back. Take it back. (*She runs over left, calling*) Hello, Lila! Hello!
      (KENNY *remains on the porch, fingering the little coin purse, with a look of conflict and misgiving on his face*)

VOICES (*Off left*)
    Come on in, kids, and meet Helen. You'll love her.
    Oh, I don't like going into people's homes.
    I've got to *go* so bad my back teeth are floating.
    I wanta get to Kanz City 'fore it gets dark.
    I've simply *got* to *go*.
      (*Now* LILA *comes on. She is an extraordinarily beautiful woman of thirty-two, blond and voluptuous, still with the form and vitality of a girl. She wears now, rather unseasonably, a leopard-skin coat, but her hair and legs are bare. One feels immediately a sincerity about her and a generosity of spirit*)

LILA Mrs. Baird!

HELEN Hello, Lila dear!
      (*The two women embrace warmly*)

LILA Oh, it's so good to see you after all these years. It's awful nice of you to take me in. It seems like you're always helping me out some way, ever since I was a little girl.

HELEN I'm delighted to see you again, Lila. Of course you're welcome.

> (RONNY CAVENDISH, *an aging juvenile actor, with obviously peroxided hair and a flamboyantly feminine personality, hurries on after* LILA)

LILA Oh, this is Ronny Cavendish, Mrs. Baird. He's our juvenile actor. Audiences just love Ronny. And he's a real pal, too.

HELEN I'm very happy to know you.

RONNY Thanks a lot. Same here, I'm sure. Lila . . .

> (RONNY *is very much in need of going to the toilet. He looks helplessly at* LILA)

LILA Would it be all right if some of my friends went inside, Mrs. Baird, to freshen up?

HELEN Of course. (*She turns back to* KENNY, *on the porch*) Kenny, would you show this gentleman inside?

RONNY Thanks a lot, I'm sure.

> (*He hurries up onto the porch.* KENNY *escorts him inside*)

LILA So that was Kenny!

HELEN Yes. Grown a little, hasn't he?

LILA You know, when I first saw him standing there, I thought for a moment he was big Kenneth. They look so much alike.

HELEN Yes. He does resemble his father. Lila, you must call me Helen now. I insist.

LILA   OK. Helen, I want you to meet two other friends of mine. Do you mind?

HELEN   I should like to.
        (LILA *turns back to the left, speaking off to the others*)

LILA   Come on, gang! (*Turns back to* HELEN) I want you to meet Madame Olga St. Valentine. Helen, She's really a very great actress. She could have been playing on Broadway all these years, but she prefers the road. (MME. OLGA *comes on, followed by* RICKY POWERS, *a sleek and handsome man with black hair and sideburns, about* LILA's *age.* MME. OLGA *is a woman of fifty, obviously an actress, wearing long, flowing garments that suggest a heroine out of Elinor Glyn's novels. She speaks in a very exaggerated British accent, dramatizing every word, every gesture.* LILA, *to* MME. OLGA) I was just telling Mrs. Baird what a wonderful actress you are, Olga.

OLGA   You mustn't listen to her, my dear lady. She exaggerates all our virtues. I'm not really as great as darling Lila would have you believe. Actually, I am just a very humble actress who happens to love her work more than life itself. More than life itself.

HELEN   I'm very honored.

LILA   And this is Ricky Powers, Helen. He plays all our heavies. That's the villains. We call 'em *heavies*. Remember when I was a kid going to the movies, I'd always get a crush on the villain? Well, Ricky and I kinda like each other offstage, don't we, Rick? But in all our shows, I always hate him. Isn't that funny?

HELEN   How do you do, Mr. Powers?

27

RICKY (*Not a very sociable man*)   How do you do?
  (KENNY *comes out now and* LILA *goes to him*)

LILA   And this is Kenny. I bet you don't remember me much, do you? Your Aunt Lila? But you just call me Lila now. I used to look after you when you were a baby. I fed you your bottle and changed your didies, and bounced you on my knee to keep you from crying. I was kind of a substitute mother for you, Kenny. But I loved you like you were my own.
  (KENNY *looks a little embarrassed*)

KENNY   Glad to meet you.

LILA   You've already met Ronny. I want you to meet the rest of my friends. This is Madame Olga St. Valentine.

OLGA (*Clasping* KENNY's *hand*)   Ah! Won't he make a splendid leading man in a few years! My boy, you're the type of young American our country needs in this tragic hour of financial doom. A fine, broad-shouldered young man who isn't afraid to face the future with honesty and courage. It gives me great hope to meet you.

KENNY (*A little unequal to her*)   Uh . . . thanks.

LILA   And, Kenny, this is Ricky Powers. Ricky's our villain, Kenny. So if you ever become our leading man, you two'll have to hate each other. (*Laughs*) But you don't have to begin now.

KENNY   Glad to meet you.

RICKY   Glad to meet you.

OLGA (*To* HELEN) My dear lady, it is most nobly generous of you to receive we poor actors, frightened refugees that we are, caught in this financial storm without a port. What a charming cottage you have. We actors are such vagabonds. We never see inside a home for years at a time. Gypsies. That's what we are. Gypsies.

RONNY (*Coming out*) You're next, Olga.
  (*A little embarrassed,* OLGA *chooses to ignore* RONNY *for the moment*)

LILA Isn't it tragic what happened to our poor tent show, Helen? Business had been bad all summer. First it was the talkies that hit us. Then the Depression. But we kept plugging along, never downhearted. We just wouldn't admit to ourselves how bad times were. Just kept telling ourselves that business'd be better in the next town. But it never was. So two nights ago, we folded. It just broke our hearts. But we're all hoping to find jobs over in Kanz City. Lotsa shows book outa there.

OLGA (*Always the optimist*) Show business isn't dead. Don't think that for a moment, dear girl. This Depression isn't going to last forever. And audiences are not going to be satisfied with talkies for very long. No. People want flesh and blood actors up there on the stage, not celluloid images. Friends keep trying to persuade *me* to go to Hollywood. They say, "Olga, they are crying for *art* out there. Art!" But I can't be persuaded. I stay faithful to my one and only love, the theatre. Maybe I'm a fool, but I can't change.

RONNY Hurry up, Olga. We gotta be getting on to Kanz City.

29

OLGA (*Glaring at* RONNY; *then, to* HELEN) If you'll be so kind as to pardon me.

>   (*Again* KENNY *shows the way as* OLGA *disappears into the house.* KENNY *returns immediately*)

RONNY I hope to God we can find jobs in Kanz City. I happen to have a friend there who runs a decorating establishment, but everyone's too poor to get decorated now. He tells me he's not making enough money to feed his cats.

LILA Ronny seems to have friends in every town we visit.

RONNY Jesus, girl, ya gotta remember I'm an old-timer. I been playin' this circuit for twenty years.

>   (HELEN *winces a little at their language*)

LILA Ricky's gonna look for me a job in Kanz City, Helen, while I stay here. Lotsa shows book outa there . . .

RONNY Mostly carnivals.

LILA Well, lotsa dramatic shows, too. Ricky's sure he'll find something, aren't ya, Rick?

RICKY Sure.

LILA He's got him a job over there already. He's having to be a bellhop at one of the hotels. Isn't that awful? A fine actor like him, having to be a bellhop? But I guess it's better'n nothing.

RICKY I told ya, baby, it's a good job to help me make connections.

RONNY I have no idea what *I'm* gonna do, but I'll find something. I never worry.

HELEN Maybe your friends would like a bite of supper, Lila. I have a few leftovers and a lovely lemon pie.

LILA No thanks, Helen. We all had a bowl of chili at the lunch counter in Pennant Junction right after I called you. We couldn't eat a thing.

RONNY No. We're not hungry. (*We may see into the kitchen now, where* MME. OLGA, *out of the bathroom, has caught sight of the lemon pie and is devouring a piece*) Where's Olga? We better be going.

HELEN Oh, don't hurry.

KENNY Mom, I'm goin' downtown.

HELEN Now don't be out late, Kenneth.

KENNY (*As though claiming a right*) This is Saturday night.

HELEN Well, I want you to take me to church in the morning.

KENNY (*Nodding to the visitors*) Glad to've met you.

LILA I'll see you later, Kenny.

RONNY (*Following* KENNY *left*) . . . and if you ever come over to Kanz City, I'll be at the Hotel Wadsworth, down by the Union Station. I should be delighted to . . .
   (OLGA *is on the porch now and perceives* RONNY's *courtship of* KENNY. *She calls in a voice that rings with authority*)

31

OLGA Ronny!
      (RONNY *is obviously respectful of* OLGA'*s authority.* KENNY
      goes off. RONNY *wanders back to* OLGA, *looking sheepish*)
Come. We must continue our journey. Weary vagabonds!
Never downhearted.

LILA Oh, I hate to see you all go.

OLGA Nonsense, child! We'll be back together in the autumn.
I feel it in my bones. I regard us all as merely between engagements. That's what I'm telling all my friends. "No, I am not
out of a job. I am only between engagements."

LILA Olga always kept our spirits up.

OLGA (*To* HELEN) Good-by, dear lady. It was most gracious
of you to receive us in your lovely home.

RONNY Yes, it was. We appreciate it.

HELEN Maybe you can visit again.

OLGA Come along, Ronny.
      (OLGA *leads the way back to the car,* RONNY *following like
      an obedient boy*)

RONNY (*Sotto voce*) What'd ya think of the house, Olga?
Could certainly stand some new draperies, don't you think?

LILA Helen, would ya mind if Ricky and I were alone for a
few minutes?

HELEN I'll be inside, Lila. Good-by, Mr. Powers. Come back
and visit us whenever you can.

32

RICKY Thanks.

(HELEN *goes inside.* LILA *and* RICKY *stand together at the doorstep*)

LILA Everything's ended now. God, I feel sad. It's like our whole world had come to an end, isn't it, Rick? A world we'd all lived in so long we'd forgotten what the resta the world was like.

RICKY You're gonna be happy here with your old friend, aren't ya?

LILA But they're not show people, Rick. Once you get used to being with show people, you feel outa place with anyone else. Just think! I haven't lived in a house like this, with a regular family, since I was a li'l girl. I can't help wondering what it's gonna be like.

RICKY Well, watch yourself and don't pull anything smart.

LILA Whatta ya mean, Rick?

RICKY You saw the way that *kid* was lookin' at ya.

LILA Rick, you're terrible.

RICKY Just a simple warning. Don't foul up the nest.

LILA Rick, sometimes I hate you. Sometimes I think you've forgotten decent people in the world really exist.

RICKY OK, OK. Forget it. (*Looking around as though to size up the town and the environment*) Overnight. Thass about all I could take of a place like this.

33

LILA Oh, I'm gonna lead a totally diff'rent kinda life while I'm here. I'm not gonna do any drinking, and I'm gonna start goin' to bed early, and I'm gonna read lotsa books, and just lead a healthy, normal existence. You know what I'm gonna do, Rick? I'm gonna read all of Shakespeare's plays while I'm here. Well, some of 'em anyway.

RICKY OK. You stay here and get highbrow. I'm goin' to Kaycee and hustle up some work.

LILA Oh God, I'm gonna miss ya, Rick.

RICKY I'm gonna miss *you*, too, baby.

LILA That's what you *say*.

RICKY I mean it, honey.

LILA If you really loved me, we'd be married by now.

RICKY There ya go on that marriage line again. Can't ya lay off?

LILA It's what I *want*, Rick. It's the *only* thing I want any more. It's the only thing that's any good.

RICKY OK, but you can count me out, see? I don't want it. Can ya get that through your head? (*She is silent*) Will you promise me never to mention it again? I don't have to get you a job, ya know. I don't have to come back for you. And I'm not gonna if you don't promise to lay off.

LILA OK, Rick. I promise.
      (*Offstage, the auto horn blows*)

RICKY Gotta beat it, baby.
(*He kisses her, then runs off*)

LILA G'by, Rick.
(*She stands watching them all drive off. Then* HELEN *appears in the doorway*)

HELEN Are your friends gone, Lila?

LILA Yes. They're gone.

HELEN Well, come in and let's get acquainted again.

LILA (*Entering the house*) Yah, it's been so long since we've seen each other.

HELEN I can't get over how you've changed.

LILA I guess life's been a lot different since you knew me, Helen. (*Seeing the davenport converted into a bed*) Is that where I sleep?

HELEN No, Lila. Kenny's going to sleep there. You're to have *his* room.

LILA (*Really pained*) Oh, Helen, I don't wanta put Kenny outa his room. Give him back his room and let *me* take the davenport.

HELEN It's all worked out, Lila. Kenny doesn't mind . . . for a while.

LILA I just can't bear the idea I'm puttin' someone out. It's just the way I am. I wish you'd let me sleep here.

35

HELEN It's all arranged, Lila. Quit worrying.

LILA Gee, your house looks good to me, Helen. You've got mosta the same furniture you had down in Oklahoma, don't ya? And look! There's the same picture of big Kenneth you kept on the mantel down there.
(LILA *takes the picture off the mantel and studies it*)

HELEN Yes. I wouldn't part with it. I've still got the watch he gave me for our fifth anniversary, too. Remember?

LILA (*Looking at the watch*) Oh, of course. You had a wonderful dinner and asked me.

HELEN It hasn't been working right lately, but I hate to part with it long enough to get it fixed. Isn't that silly?

LILA (*Returning to* KENNETH's *picture*) Wasn't he handsome? I never told you, Helen, but I guess I can now. I had the wildest crush on your husband that a silly, young girl could possibly have. (HELEN *smiles*) He was my model. I told myself that I was gonna have a husband like him some day. And I measured every man I met by your Kenneth. I'd ask myself, "Is he as nice and intelligent as Mr. Baird? Is he as honest? Is he as thoughtful and understanding? Is he as strong and handsome?" I didn't often answer any of those questions with a yes, but I tried. I guess lotsa times I've tried to talk myself into thinking some guys are better than they really are.

HELEN I'm sorry your marriage to Ed Comiskey didn't work out well for you.

LILA (*A little reluctant to say more*) Well . . . I'll tell ya all about it some time. (*Changing the subject*) How come you

36

moved away from Oklahoma, Helen? After big Kenneth died?

HELEN This was our home. This is where we met and got married. I had more friends here, and I thought Kenny and I might need their help. We were managing fine until the Depression hit. Then I was glad for my nurse's training. I took a job out at the city hospital.

LILA Oh, you're a nurse now?

HELEN Yes. And Kenny got a good job at a filling station in town, right after he graduated from high school. We're getting along fine now.

LILA Oh, I'm glad. It don't seem right for people like you to be poor.

HELEN We were never really wealthy, Lila, but down in Oklahoma, Kenneth kept us pretty comfortable.

LILA How'd he die, Helen?

HELEN I hate to be reminded, Lila.

LILA Oh, I'm sorry, Helen. Forget I asked you . . .

HELEN Didn't your mother write you about it?

LILA She wrote me she'd been to the funeral, then I didn't hear again.

HELEN He gave his life for another.

LILA How?

HELEN   He was elected to the school board after you left. Every
year, we attended the school picnic together and the students
always wanted to go swimming. One year we warned them
against it because the river was swollen after the spring rains,
and the currents were dangerous.

LILA   Oh, I remember how treacherous that old river was.

HELEN   But the young people wouldn't listen to us. They said
the picnic wouldn't be a success if they didn't get to go swimming. There was nothing we could do to prevent them. Then
one of the girls got carried downstream and was about to
drown. She was the brightest girl in the whole school. She
graduated three weeks later, valedictorian of her class. But
Kenenth drowned in saving her.

LILA   (*Feeling empathic pain*)   Oh, Helen!

HELEN   I was nearly out of my wits with grief. Death, when it
comes like Kenneth's did, seems like such an injustice that
you can't believe in a god who'd let it happen.

LILA   I know just how you feel.

HELEN   But God can't prevent death. He can only help us to
accept it. I finally learned that. We're put here like the ani-
mals of the earth, Lila, and we have to bear the same natural
misfortunes they do. Only God can help us to survive them.

LILA   (*To herself*)   He gave his life for another.

HELEN   I'm happy to say that the girl has proved worthy. She
graduated from college with honors and works now in a wel-
fare agency. She writes me once in a while.

38

LILA   Oh, if I'd ever lost a husband like Mr. Baird, I don't think I ever would have got over it.

HELEN   Time helps a little. And Kenny! There are my hopes for Kenny.

LILA   It must make you feel good that Kenny looks so much like his father. It must make you feel sometimes that he *is* his father.

HELEN   (*Troubled*)   Well . . . no. I never let myself think that.

LILA   Anyway, you had a nice husband once, Helen. You can be thankful for that.

HELEN   I am.

LILA   Ed Comiskey was a very big disappointment to me, Helen. I'll tell you that much right now.

HELEN   I'm sorry.

LILA   But I guess I couldn't have expected to find anyone like Mr. Baird in a tent show.

HELEN   (*Trying to be brighter*)   Are you in love with this . . . what's his name . . . Ricky?

LILA   (*Modestly*)   Well, he's nothing like Mr. Baird. He's got a lotta faults, but . . . I have to have *some*one, Helen. I just die if I don't have someone to kinda lean on. And he shows me a good time.

HELEN   He's very handsome.

LILA   Yeh. He is, isn't he? I always like handsome men.

HELEN   That's understandable.

LILA   Maybe that's all you can say for Ricky. He's not very reliable, and he's got an awful temper.

HELEN   How long have you known him?

LILA   He joined the show a couple a years ago. Madame Olga found him once when we were in Gary, Indiana. She took him into the show and had kind of a crush on him for a while, and then he started dating me. Madame Olga was furious and wouldn't speak to me for a long time, but finally we made it up.

HELEN   You mean . . . Madame Olga and Ricky were . . . sweethearts?

LILA   For a while.

HELEN   Well, you've grown accustomed to much different people since I knew you, haven't you, Lila?

LILA   But if you knew them better, Helen, I'm sure you'd like them.

HELEN   Well, you probably want to be getting unpacked.

LILA   Oh, it's early yet. Gee, I could sit and talk for hours.

HELEN   I'm afraid I'll have to save the rest of our talk for morning, Lila. I've been working all day and I'm tired. I'm going to have to turn in.

LILA   Oh sure. Don't let me keep you up.

HELEN   My, that's a pretty fur coat.

LILA   That's my proudest possession. I bought it when we were in St. Louis last fall. It took all my savings. It's about all I got to show for all the years I been in show business. I'm gonna have to put it in a cedar bag now for the summer. I'll miss it so. I wish I could wear it all summer long.

HELEN   The bath is down the hall. You can get to it from your room without coming through here. There's plenty of hot water if you want a bath.

LILA   OK. Sometimes, when I don't sleep, I get up and fix myself a glass of hot milk or something, Helen. Is that all right?

HELEN   Sure. My room is clear at the back of the house. You won't disturb me. And Kenny sleeps like the dead. I hope you don't object to the music from that awful skating rink.

LILA   No. I kinda like it. Makes me feel right at home.

HELEN   (*Smiles benignly*)   Good night, Lila.

LILA   Good night, Helen. I wanta tell ya again how nice it is of you to let me stay. I really don't know where I coulda gone if it hadn't been for you. But I can still help you around the house, Helen, like I did when I was a girl. I can cook and clean for you whenever you want me to, and not be in the way.

HELEN   You have a good rest first. (*Turning on a small lamp*) I always leave this little light on for Kenny. Sometimes, he's out rather late.

41

LILA I'll remember.

HELEN Good night.

LILA Good night, Helen.
(HELEN *exits through dining room into hallway that leads to the back of the house. Alone,* LILA *lights a cigarette and looks about the room as though in wonder at her new home. Again, she studies the picture of big Kenneth on the mantelpiece. She seems extremely sad. Finally she goes to the window to hear the grinding music from the skating rink, which fills the air with manufactured gaiety. It brings a smile to her face, as though she had found something familiar*)

Curtain

Scene Two

It is about two hours later. LILA *has unpacked and is in bed, asleep. The night outside is black, with dim illumination from a nearby street lamp and from the small table lamp lighted for* KENNY. *The skating rink closed at midnight, an hour or so earlier. Now we hear the sounds of drunken revelry from* KENNY *and* JELLY, *returning home, singing raucously.* KENNY, *however, stops singing as they near his house.*

KENNY Hey, quiet down. You wanta wake up my mom?

JELLY Oh . . . p-pardon me for living.

KENNY What we need is a car. Ya can't pick up girls without a car. Thass all girls are interested in, is a car. They don't even care who's driving it, just as long as there's a set of wheels to take 'em someplace. They don't even care where you take 'em, just as long as you take 'em there in a car.
(THEY *drop to the doorstep and* KENNY *takes a long swallow from a half-pint bottle of whiskey he draws from his pocket. Then he passes it to* JELLY)

JELLY I don't want any more, Ken.

KENNY There *isn't* any more. Just lose this on your way home.

JELLY Oh, OK. (JELLY *accepts the bottle and* KENNY *rises unsteadily to his feet,* JELLY *noticing*) Hey, you're drunk, Ken.

43

KENNY   So what?

JELLY   You better let me help ya inside.

KENNY   (*Staggering to the door*)   I'll be OK.

JELLY   Well . . . see ya tomorrow.
(JELLY *runs off.* KENNY *gets into the house and manages to turn off the table lamp. Then, forgetting the arrival of* LILA, *he stumbles into his own room and begins to undress, unbuttoning his coveralls, letting them fall to the floor, trying to jerk them over his shoes. He loses balance and falls.* LILA *awakens and calls out frightenedly*)

LILA   Who's there?

KENNY   (*To himself*)   Jesus Christ! I forgot.

LILA   Kenny! Is that you?

KENNY   Yah!

LILA   Is something the matter?

KENNY   (*Trying to get to his feet*)   I forgot, Lila. I forgot you were here. I'm awful God damn sorry, Lila. I really did forget.
(*He finally makes it in to his new bed*)

LILA   (*Following*)   Are you all right, Kenny?

KENNY   (*Getting off his coveralls now, throwing them into a corner, hiding himself in bed*)   Yah. I'm aw right. I forgot you were there. No kiddin'.

44

LILA That's all right, Kenny. (*Closer to him, she smells his breath*) Why, Kenny Baird, you're drunk!

KENNY I just had one little drink downtown with some a the fellas. Thass all, Lila. I swear to God.

LILA You don't have to apologize to *me*, Kenny. I'm not your mother.

KENNY (*Free of guilt now, he begins to laugh*) Yah. I forgot.

LILA Are ya sick or anything?

KENNY Naw, I'm OK, Lila.

LILA (*Starting back to her room*) Well, if ya need anything, just holler.

KENNY Lila . . . you're not gonna tell Mom, or anything, are ya?

LILA Course not.

KENNY On your Girl Scout honor?

LILA (*Laughing*) On my Girl Scout honor.

KENNY I'm beginning to remember more about you now, Lila. The way you took care a me when I was a kid. Mom was kinda strict but you'd gimme anything I wanted. You were swell.

LILA Yah. I'm a softie. (*Just notices he hasn't taken off his shoes*) Kenny! your shoes!

KENNY Oh . . . yah. (*He sticks his feet from under the covers and she takes off his shoes and socks*)

LILA Have ya got any pajamas?

KENNY Don't wear 'em. You wanta know something, Lila? You sure are good-lookin'.

LILA Thanks, Kenny.

KENNY I mean it. That guy Ricky. Is he your boy friend, Lila?

LILA Yah.

KENNY I guess it's none a my business but I din much like him.

LILA I din think you would.

KENNY As a matter of fact, I thought all those people you were with were pretty darn peculiar.

LILA Ya did? Well . . . they're show people, Kenny. I guess maybe show people *are* a little peculiar. Go to sleep now, Kenny.

KENNY Lila . . . I hear actresses are all real wild.

LILA Go to sleep, Kenny.

KENNY Lila, when I was a kid, you used to kiss me good night. I remember.

LILA Well . . . you're not a kid any more. (*She starts for her room but he grabs her by the hand and holds her*)

46

KENNY Aren't ya gonna kiss me good night, Lila?

LILA (*Sweetly*) No, Kenny.

KENNY Aw, c'mon, Lila.

LILA (*Firmly*) Go to sleep, Kenny.
>   (*She hurries inside her room now, closing the door between them, sitting on her bed a little shaken*)

KENNY (*Groaning*) Aw, Lila!
>   (*He sits up for a moment, feeling sore, then falls off to sleep, snoring rhapsodically.* LILA, *however, is rather disturbed*)

Curtain

Scene Three

It is rather late the next morning, a Sunday. Church bells sound melodiously in the distance. KENNY *is sunk in heavy sleep; and, on the porch,* LILA *and* HELEN *sit, having their second cup of breakfast coffee. On the floor of the porch are the Sunday papers.*

LILA   Helen, I can't really tell you what my marriage to Ed Comiskey was like. You've never known people like those Comiskey brothers. They're just out of another world entirely. You wouldn't believe the things I told you.

HELEN   He seemed like a nice young man when I met him.

LILA   Oh, Ed was nice. But there were . . . complications.

HELEN   Was he . . . *peculiar* in some way?

LILA   Oh no. Ed was very sweet to me. But he was weak. You see, the other Comiskey, Vincent, was not Ed's real brother. No. They called their show the Comiskey Brothers Comedians, but Vincent wasn't Ed's brother at all. Vincent was Ed's *father*.

HELEN (*Appalled*)   No!

LILA   . . . But I din know it for quite a while after we were married. Then I found out that old Vincent Comiskey dyed his hair to keep the gray from showing. He wanted to stay

48

young and keep on playing the leading man. Vincent was the real boss of the show. And a few months after we were married, he started sending Ed out on booking trips . . . Ed wasn't a very good actor. And then, when Ed was gone, old Vincent started coming to my room, trying to force himself on me.

HELEN Your husband's *father?*

LILA I told you you'd never heard of people like them. Oh, he was a horrible old man. I just couldn't stand him. He tried to force me to make love to him . . . in all sorts of intimate ways that . . . that just made me sick, Helen.

HELEN Well, I'd have gone straight to his wife and told her that . . .

LILA Oh, Mrs. Comiskey knew all about him. She din care what he did. She was in love with another man, a man who played the xylophone between the acts, and he had a wife, too, and two little kids.

HELEN Oh, that's shocking.

LILA And the xylophone player's wife was in love with the crew boss, the man who had charge of putting up the tent and taking it down.

HELEN I've never heard of such people.

LILA I told you you wouldn't believe me.

HELEN Then you should have reported that Mr. Comiskey to the police. The man was a degenerate.

49

LILA But we were in a new town every week, Helen, and I never knew anyone. But old Vincent knew everyone in every town we went to. And people just loved him, too. He was what you'd call a "hail fellow well met," and he'd speak at the Rotary Clubs and the Kiwanis, every town we were in. I couldn't have gone to the police and told them to arrest Vincent Comiskey. The police would have arrested me for being a trouble-maker.

HELEN But you told Ed, I hope.

LILA I tried to tell him after he got back from his first booking trip, but he wouldn't believe me.

HELEN (*Appalled*) He wouldn't?

LILA He didn't wanta believe me. He was scared of his father, and he wouldn't have known how to protect me. It . . . almost made me sorry for Ed.

HELEN Oh, Lila, I feel guilty now for ever having advised you to marry him.

LILA *You* couldn't have known all that would happen. Living back there in that little Oklahoma town where everybody was so honest and friendly, we never guessed there were people like Vincent Comiskey in the world.

HELEN Vincent Comiskey doesn't sound any worse to me than your stepbrother Harry.

LILA Well, no . . . I guess you're right. I just couldn't have kept on living in the same house with Harry any longer.

HELEN (*With extreme contempt*) A beast of a man!

LILA Sometimes I get the feeling all men are like that.

HELEN What did you finally do, Lila?

LILA I just ran away one day. I hardly knew what I was doing, I was so fearful and anxious; but I managed to get on a train somehow, and ended up in Bismarck, North Dakota, in the middle of winter. I just locked myself up in a hotel room and din see anyone, I felt so terrible. Then . . . some people found me.

HELEN (*Puzzled*) *Found* you?

LILA Well, I . . . I guess I'd tried to kill myself, Helen.

HELEN (*Shocked*) Lila!

LILA Oh now, don't sound so horrified, Helen. I din really mean it. It was just a half-hearted attempt I made, with some sleeping medicine a doctor gave me. It's never gonna happen again. I've learned a lot since then. They took me to a big hospital, a . . . a mental institution. Oh, it scared me to go to such a place, but after I'd been there awhile, I began to feel a lot different. They kept me there for three months, seeing a doctor, and making pottery and sewing. I learned a lot from that doctor. Men don't scare me any more, like they did then. I was just too goody-good in lotsa ways, Helen.

HELEN Lila, why didn't you let someone know where you were?

LILA Why? No one coulda helped me.

HELEN Just the same . . .

LILA And the snow was so deep all winter, our Sunday visitors couldn't even get to us, mosta the time.

HELEN Surely you wrote to your mother.

LILA *Why,* Helen? Imagine Mama getting a postcard saying, "Dear Mama, I'm in the loony bin. Love, Lila." Why, they'da had to take her to one, too. No. I just wrote Mama that I was visiting a friend up in North Dakota. She musta wondered where I ever met anyone in North Dakota, but I guess Mama wondered about a lotta things in my life. I'm kinda relieved she's dead now. I don't feel I have to account to anyone any more.

HELEN Lila, I'm so sorry for you.

LILA Why? The hospital wasn't a bad place. As a matter of fact, there's times when I wouldn't mind being back.

HELEN (*Repelled*) Lila! No!

LILA Oh, you don't have to worry, Helen. I'm not ever going back. And I'm never gonna do anything silly again with that darn sleeping medicine. This doctor, he made me see things a lot differently. He told me I was "emotionally immature." He said lots of people are. He said that "immature" people expect the whole world to be rosy, and when they have to face *reality,* it looks hard and ugly. So, I just don't expect so much a life any more, Helen. And I been gettin' along just fine. I don't fight things like I used to. I've learned to take things as they come and make the best of them.

HELEN I suppose that's what we all have to do.

52

LILA Sure. Like this Depression. We just gotta make the best of it.

HELEN (*Rising*) Well, it's time I was getting ready for church. Would you like to go with me?

LILA *Me?* In church?

HELEN Why not?

LILA I wouldn't know how to act.

HELEN Why should you feel such a stranger in church?

LILA Church is for people who are good already, Helen. I . . . I believe in God and everything, but . . . I'm not very holy.

HELEN All right. I don't insist. (*Starts inside*) I have a feeling I won't be able to get Kenny to go with me, either. (*At the door, she turns back to* LILA) What time did Kenny get in last night? Did you hear him?

LILA Oh no.

HELEN (*She returns to* LILA *now, speaking in a very confidential voice*) Lila . . . Kenny worries me . . . sometimes he comes home drunk.

LILA (*All innocence*) Oh . . . he does?

HELEN It's hard raising a son, Lila.

LILA Yah.

HELEN A son . . . without a father.

LILA Oh, Kenny's gonna turn into just as fine a man as his dad. You know he is.

HELEN No. I *don't* know that. (*She is inscrutably silent for a moment*) I . . . I'm very disappointed in Kenny. In some ways.

LILA Honest?

HELEN He drinks, like I told you. Oh, not often, but often enough. And . . . he goes out with the trashiest girls in town. Oh, it kills me.

LILA Oh . . . (*She wonders if* HELEN *probably would not consider her a "trashy girl"*) Well, he'll get over that, Helen. He'll fall in love some day and . . .

HELEN I sometimes wonder if he's capable.

LILA Oh, of course he is!

HELEN I mean, of falling in love. Some people aren't, you know. Some people just look for gratification in their mates. Purely animal. Kenny has never shown any real heart interest in any of the girls he sees. I don't even *know* the girls he sees. I never see them.

LILA Lotsa boys are like that when they're his age, Helen. It's because they're young and just wanta enjoy themselves. He'll get over it.

HELEN There's something else I have to tell you. (*She peeks inside the door again to make sure* KENNY *is still asleep, and then continues in a very confidential voice*) He doesn't *steal,* Lila, but . . . sometimes he *takes* things.

LILA (*Quite shocked but trying not to show it*) Honest?

HELEN I can't get him to talk about it, or even admit it. He acts like he didn't even know he did it. But he does. He's been doing it now for several years. It started out his first year of high school. He had a music teacher, very young and pretty, and he walked off one time with a pair of her gloves. Isn't that puzzling? Gloves. He never takes anything that's worth much, never takes money, or jewelry. But if you do find anything missing, let me know.

LILA (*Light-heartedly*) I don't have anything valuable but the fur coat. Except for that, he can have anything I've got.

HELEN It's the principle, Lila.

LILA Sure.

HELEN It worries me to death. It makes me feel I've failed him in some way, but I don't know how.

LILA It isn't *your* fault, Helen.

HELEN I so wish I could afford to send him away to college, to prepare him for a respectable place in life. But I can't. He's good at his work, though. He seems to know everything about cars and machinery. Most of the well-to-do men in town take their cars to the station for Kenny to work on. They pay him extra, too. And just a couple of months ago, he was offered a very good job at one of the air plants over in Wichita.

55

They'd put him to work and teach him at the same time, at a very good salary for these times. I did my best to persuade him to take it. There's going to be a future in aeronautics, for certain. But . . . (*She expresses a feeling of helplessness*) . . . he wouldn't take the job.

LILA Why not?

HELEN Oh, he made up a lot of reasons, but the truth of it is . . . Kenny just doesn't want to leave home.

LILA That's funny.

HELEN Most boys his age would have jumped to get such a job, but Kenny acted perfectly unconcerned, and turned it down like a bag of peanuts. He doesn't seem to have any desire at all to make something of his life.

LILA Don't worry, Helen.

HELEN A young man's life seems to me such a precious thing. Oh, I have the feeling now that Kenny is at a turning point where he could grow into a strong, honest man like his father, or . . . an evil man, either one. And I don't expect him to be a *great* man, or a very religious one, necessarily. But I want him to be *good* in the way that will make him understand people, and be reasonable in life, with a sense of justice, and a concern for others. That's all I'm asking. There are so few good men in the world.

LILA (*In a voice that knows*) Yah!

HELEN People get so twisted by envy and greed and cheap ambition.

56

LILA   Yah! I know.

HELEN   And I love him so. After his father died, Kenny was all I had, and he became too important to me, I fear. But I pray for him to turn out well. And I get so anxious about him at times that I perhaps bungle things and do the very thing I shouldn't. I feel a terrible responsibility.

LILA   Didn't you ever think of marrying again, Helen?

HELEN   Yes. I thought of it . . . once.

LILA   Did you meet someone you liked?

HELEN   There was a young farmer here, when Kenny and I first moved back from Oklahoma. His name was Swede. We were very fond of each other, but . . . Kenny hated him.

LILA   Why?

HELEN   Children can be jealous as monsters, Lila. Kenny just wouldn't stand for another man being in the house. He was only nine or ten at the time, but he was ready to fight Swede, he was so jealous.

LILA   Honest?

HELEN   Swede promised to straighten Kenny out if I married him, and maybe that's just what Kenny needed. But I was afraid. I made my choice. I told Swede not to come back any more. Maybe I was wrong.

LILA   Kenny woulda accepted it in time.

HELEN   But he made me feel so guilty, like I was deserting him. I couldn't stand the accusing look in his eyes when Swede came to call. It's the only time in my life I felt weak.

LILA   You both seem so happy here, I wouldn't a dreamed you had these troubles.

HELEN   You mustn't brood about what I've told you, Lila. Things can work themselves out. I've faith in that.

LILA   Oh sure.

HELEN   I'm going to try to get the little dickens out of bed now to take me to church, but I may not succeed. (*She goes inside and takes* KENNY *by the shoulder*) Kenny! (*He doesn't stir*) Kenny, are you awake? (*No answer*) Kenny, it's late. You've slept long enough. I want you to take me to church. (*A very noticeable silence*) Kenny, you're awake now. I can tell. You just don't want to go to church. It wouldn't hurt you a bit to take me to church. Kenny. It wouldn't hurt you a bit. (*No answer*) Very well. I'll go alone and atone for all our sins. But let me see you up and dressed by the time I get back.
   (*She goes back to her room now as* LILA *comes in from the porch.* KENNY *cautiously opens one eye to peek at her with, and then whispers hoarsely*)

KENNY   Hi!

LILA (*Whispering*)   Hi! How do ya feel?

KENNY   OK. Why?

LILA   No hangover?

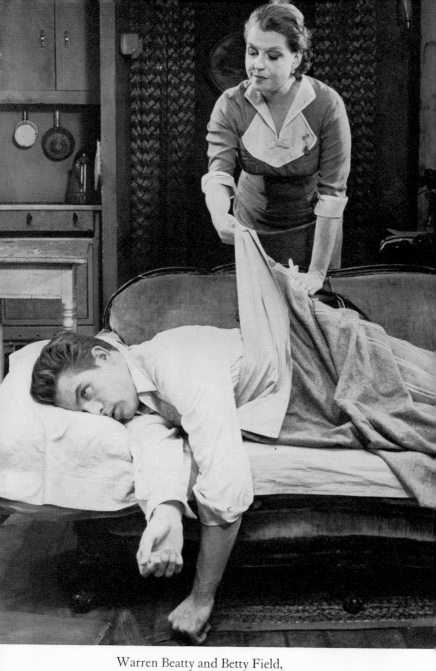

Warren Beatty and Betty Field,
as HELEN and KENNY BAIRD

KENNY   How'd *you* know?

LILA   I helped you out last night.

KENNY   Ya did? Gee, I don't remember anything. Did you tell
Mom?

LILA   Now, what do you take me for?

KENNY *(Smiles)*   Thanks.

LILA   Don't mention it.

KENNY   I guess I do have a kind of a headache. I could sure use
a cup of coffee.

LILA *(Hurrying to the kitchen)*   Coming right up. (KENNY
lifts himself to light a cigarette, and LILA *is back almost im-
mediately with a cup of black coffee)* Here y'are. *(Digs into
her purse)* Here's a couple a aspirin, too.

KENNY   Gee, you think a everything, don'tcha?

LILA   Just about.
   (We hear HELEN's *voice again from the back room)*

HELEN   Oh, I'm late. My watch stopped on me again. I declare.
I'm going to have to hurry. *(Before she gets back to the living
room,* LILA *has taken* KENNY's *cup and cigarette and is using
them as her own, while* KENNY *slips under the covers again
and feigns sleep.* HELEN *looks at him)* Possum! Playing possum!

LILA   I'll clean up in the kitchen, Helen.

HELEN   And look at the roast, too, Lila. Don't let it get dry.

LILA   Sure.

HELEN   I'll look in on Mrs. Mulvaney to see if she wants to go to church, too. She's my neighbor lady, but she's almost as much a widow as I am. Her husband's a traveling salesman, and when he's home she doesn't go to church. She doesn't want to leave him. I can't blame her. Maybe religion is useless to people who are happy together. I know I didn't get much out of church before Kenneth died. Now . . . I don't know what I'd do without it. (*She puts on her hat and starts for the door*) If Kenny wants breakfast, do anything to keep him from going into the kitchen. He wrecks it every time he gets a glass of water.

LILA   I'll fix him something.

HELEN   Don't pamper him. When he gets up late he doesn't deserve a big breakfast. Well, good-by, you sinners!
     (HELEN *exits*)

LILA   G'by, Helen.
     (KENNY *stirs again*)

KENNY   Was I all right last night, Lila? I mean . . . Did I do anything I shouldn't have?

LILA   You were awful drunk.

KENNY   (*Taking back his coffee and cigarette*)   Yah, I know.

LILA   Apart from that, you were a perfect gentleman.

60

KENNY Me? A perfect gentleman? (*He laughs*) Hey, Lila, tell me about those shows you were in. What'd ya do in 'em?

LILA Why, I acted, silly.

KENNY Whatta ya do when y'*act*, Lila? I mean, how do ya do it?

LILA Ya just make believe you're someone else. Ya make believe for serious.

KENNY I don't see how anyone can do that. Where were these shows? What was the name of them?

LILA Well, when I left your folks down in Oklahoma, I went off with the Comiskey Brothers Comedians. I stayed with them a year and then I was sick for a while, up in North Dakota. And when I got well, I came down to Des Moines and got a job with the Daisy Curtis Funmakers.

KENNY The Daisy Curtis Funmakers?

LILA Yah. Daisy Curtis used to work for the Comiskeys as a soubrette, but they had a fight and she left. That was before I got sick. She told me when she left that if I ever needed a job to look her up, so I did. It was kind of a vaudeville show she had, playing movie houses all through Iowa and Nebraska. Business was good, too. That was before the Depression. You should have seen Daisy. Onstage, she was very pretty. Wore a beautiful wig and lovely gowns. But offstage, she looked awful funny. Cut her hair just like a man, and wore pants, and smoked cigars, and swore just like a sailor. She was good-hearted, though. She was good to me and I liked her. I like anyone who's good to me.

KENNY   How long'd that job last?

LILA   About two years, till I got a better one with Gladys Boomer and Her Texas Blondes.

KENNY   The movie actress?

LILA   She is now but wasn't then. It was an all-girl show. Her mother ran it. We played almost every state west of the Mississippi. I sang and danced and . . .

KENNY   How? Show me.

LILA   Oh, something like this.
(*She does a few dance steps to illustrate;* KENNY *is aware of every move she makes*)

KENNY (*When she stops*)   Go on. Let's see some more.

LILA   Oh, I'm winded. I haven't danced for a long time and I'm outa practice. Well, I stayed with Gladys Boomer for three years, till her mother took her out to Hollywood and got her in pictures. Now she's very big-time. Her mother really pushed her. I wrote her once asking her if there was anything in Hollywood for me, but . . . she never answered my letter.

KENNY   Snubbed ya, huh?

LILA   Well, when ya get famous, ya get awful busy, I guess.

KENNY   Think *you* might be in movies some day?

LILA   Well . . . stranger things have happened.

KENNY   Gee, that'd be swell, wouldn't it?

LILA   It sure would.

KENNY   Then you'd probably snub *us*, Mom and me.

LILA   I would not, Kenny. I wouldn't snub *any*one. I'd be just as loyal to my friends as ever.

KENNY   (*He may be baiting her a little*)   OK. Then what happened?

LILA   Then I got an acting job with Henry Weisman's Gypsies. And then came the Depression. And here I am, wondering if I'll ever work again.

KENNY   Ya ever think of doing anything but acting?

LILA   Oh, I couldn't give up show business. It's in my very blood. Besides, there's nothing else I know how to do.

KENNY   Don't you know shorthand and typing?

LILA   No. When I was in high school, I stayed away from all those *hard* courses. I took things like acting and glee club and cooking and sewing. Those courses were fun. And I guess . . . I always wanted the fun outa life.

KENNY   Who doesn't?
       (*They laugh together*)

LILA   Besides, I'm a very good actress. You should have seen me in *Smilin' Through*. That was my best part. Oh, that play had such a sad ending. You see, I played an old-fashioned kind of girl in it, and wore a great hoopskirt made of white lace. And the villain in the play . . . Ricky played the part

. . . was going to shoot the man I loved. And I couldn't bear for the man I loved to die so I ran between him and the bullet and Ricky shot me right through the heart . . . (*She has begun to believe in the scene and re-enacts it*) . . . and then I sank into my lover's arms and died.

KENNY I saw that in the movies with Norma Shearer. I don't like those sad pictures.

LILA You don't?

KENNY No. I like Westerns.

LILA Some of my friends said I was just as good as Norma Shearer, and they meant it, too.

KENNY Gee, I'm beginning to feel kinda hungry.

LILA (*Playing a servant's role now*) What would you care for, sir?

KENNY Some tomato juice?

LILA And what else, sir?

KENNY (*Playing it like a king*) Oh . . . how about some pancakes?

LILA (*A little dismayed*) Pancakes?

KENNY Do you know how to make 'em, Lila?

LILA Yah!

KENNY Would they be too much trouble?

LILA I guess I can manage.

KENNY And some sausage?

LILA Sure. I can fix some sausage.

KENNY Gee, that'd be swell, Lila.

LILA Sure. Tomato juice, pancakes, sausage. Coming right up!

> (*She departs for kitchen, singing "Lookin' at the World Through Rose-Colored Glasses," happy as a lark.* KENNY *leans back in his bed, with a smile of gratification on his face*)

KENNY Ya wanta know something, Lila? I'm gonna like having you here.

Curtain

ACT TWO

Scene One

It is a month later. Summer is close to an end now. The trees about the house are just beginning to turn, and the rose bushes are heavy with flowers. It is late afternoon, or early evening, and LILA, *dressed most becomingly, sits on the front doorstep sipping a cocktail out of a small cheese glass, enjoying the beauty of the setting sun and the quiet of the twilight atmosphere. Presently she lifts her eyes and looks down the street to see* KENNY *on his way home from the filling station. A sweet smile comes over her face as she anticipates his coming. She speaks melodiously.*

LILA   Good evening, Mr. Kenny Baird!

KENNY (*Smiling, too*)   Hi, Lila!

LILA   You look like you'd been workin' hard today.

KENNY   Workin' hard doin' nothin'. Sittin' on my tail mosta the afternoon.

LILA   No business?

KENNY   Too hot. No customers. Whatcha drinkin' there?

LILA   It's a little julep I fix myself once in a while. I had a bottle of rum in my suitcase that Ricky brought me from Cuba a long time ago. I thought I'd make us a few cocktails tonight to help celebrate your mother's anniversary.

69

KENNY (*Bringing a small package out of his pocket*)   I brought her a present.

LILA   Oh, isn't it wrapped pretty? Did *you* wrap it up like that?

KENNY   No. They did that down at the jewelry store. Who do you think I am, Michelangelo?

LILA   What'd ya get her, Kenny?

KENNY (*Handing her the receipt*)   That's what I gave her. That's the receipt.

LILA (*Reading*)   A Hamilton wrist watch, fifty-five dollars and eighty cents, bought and paid for. Oh, Kenny! It's wonderful of you to be so thoughtful.

KENNY   Well . . . I always wanted to do something nice for Mom. I mean . . . I've always felt like I owed her something.

LILA   Why, Kenny?

KENNY   Well, she coulda got married again, if it hadn't been for me.

LILA   Did she ever tell you she was sorry she didn't get married? Or blame you?

KENNY   No, of course not. But I feel sorry for her now, without a husband to do things for her. I try to make up in any way I can. This is the first job I ever had that gave me a chance to save enough to buy her something. I know she's been needing a watch, and so . . . I been saving since June.

LILA Kenny, I'd never a suspected you had such thoughtful feelings.

KENNY Well, I think a lot of Mom. I guess I don't always show it. I mean, we're always scrapping. I don't know why. It's crazy, isn't it, when two people who really like each other can't keep from fighting?

LILA Yeh.

KENNY Anyway, Mom and I have been through a lot together, and I . . . Well, I appreciate her.

LILA She'll be thrilled with the present, Kenny.

KENNY I hope so. Now! how about one of those fancy drinks you mixed?
    (KENNY *leads the way inside the house and* LILA *follows. In the living room, he places his mother's present in a table drawer*)

LILA OK. If you think Helen wouldn't mind.

KENNY (*Hotly*) What business is it of hers if I take a drink?

LILA I just don't want her to get mad at *me*. I don't want her to think I'm a bad influence.

KENNY (*A little sarcastic*) Yah. No bad influences.
    (*He tastes his drink*)

LILA Ya like it?

KENNY It's OK.

LILA   I like nice sweet drinks that taste good. I never did like those old bitter drinks, like martinis. I like things always to be sweet as possible.

KENNY   I guess . . . I'd rather have a beer. (*He goes to kitchen for a bottle of beer*) Mmmmm, dinner sure smells good.

LILA   (*Turning on the radio, getting a program of sweet dance music*) Oh, I've been cooking all afternoon. There's a chicken in the oven, and some scalloped potatoes, and an angel food cake.

KENNY   (*Seeing the cake on a shelf*)   Damn, that looks good.

LILA   Now, Kenny, please don't eat any of that until dinner. *Please!*

KENNY   OK. Don't get yourself in an uproar. (*Returns with a bottle of beer*) Lila?

LILA   Yah?

KENNY   (*Suddenly serious now*)   I s'pose Mom has told you about . . . some of my bad habits.

LILA   Whatta ya mean, Kenny?

KENNY   I haven't always paid for the things I've . . . taken.

LILA   Things like that are none of my business, Kenny.

KENNY   What makes a man do things like that, Lila? *Take* things that don't really belong to him.

LILA   I dunno.

KENNY   It's kinda childish, isn't it? Sometimes I feel embarrassed as hell when I think about it.

LILA   Ya don't do it any more, do you, Kenny?

KENNY   Not for quite a while.

LILA   How come ya told me about it, Kenny?

KENNY   I just felt I could. You never criticize people.

LILA   No.

KENNY   I always wanted to tell someone.

LILA   Now forget it. This is a party, and there's nice dance music on the radio.

KENNY   From the cocktail lounge at the Hotel Muehlbach over in Kaycee.

LILA   Let's you and me pretend we're steppin' out tonight, shall we, Kenny?

KENNY   Like how?

LILA   Well, I happen to be a very socially prominent young lady in Kanz City. My father has been trying to persuade me for months to marry a man I don't like, but Father says I've *got* to marry him because his family is very prominent, too, and I am miserably unhappy. Because, actually, I love a young student who doesn't have any money at all. That's you.

KENNY   (*A little amused*)   OK., I'm a poor student.

73

LILA   . . . And I have just run away from a big party out at the country club and come down to the Muehlbach to meet you. And when we meet, you say, "Lila darling, it's *divine* to see you again."

KENNY   (*Playing along*) "Lila darling, it's *divine* to see you again."

LILA   And I rush into your arms, and I say, "Kenneth dearest, I've missed you so terribly."

KENNY   Then I say, "Let's beat it and get a beer."

LILA   No, you don't. You take me into your arms to dance.

KENNY   In my dirty coveralls?

LILA   Oh, I don't mind about things like that. I'm very wealthy and very socially prominent, but I'm not a snob.

KENNY   OK. So I take you into my arms to dance, and plant a big smackeroo right on your kisser.
(*He grabs her to him and kisses her on the lips.* LILA *is astounded*)

LILA   Kenny!

KENNY   Well, isn't that what he'd do? This young student you're so nuts about.

LILA   Well . . . not right in the middle of the cocktail lounge where everybody can see.

KENNY   Oh, sure, this young student, he's very impulsive. He doesn't care what people think.

LILA (*A little sad*)   Kenny!

KENNY   And then he says, "Lila darling, I've got a little room in an attic, where we can be alone together. How about it, Lila?"

LILA (*Turning from him*)   Now stop it, Kenny.

KENNY   Come on. Aren't we playing any more?

LILA   No. I don't think we better play any more.

KENNY   Why not? The game's just getting good.
    (*He goes to her again and grabs her in his arms*)

LILA   Kenny!

KENNY   You started it, for crying out loud!
    (*He kisses her again*)

LIL   Kenny! Don't! You mustn't do that, Kenny.
    (*She tears loose from him*)

KENNY   Why not?

LILA   Kenny, it isn't right.

KENNY   You used to kiss me when I was a baby, din ya?

LILA   That's different.

KENNY   ... And cuddle me in your arms. What's wrong with what we're doin' now? Why not? You're not my real aunt.

LILA   No. But I'm a lot older'n you.

KENNY   You don't act it. You don't look it, either. You don't seem any older to me than the girls I went to school with.

LILA   Don't I, Kenny?

KENNY   Of course not . . . except maybe ya got more sense.

LILA   Kenny, I wouldn't do anything like that with you. What'd Helen say?

KENNY   (*Hotly*)   I don't live my life thinking what Mother'd say.

LILA   But how'd I feel, Kenny, if Helen found out there was anything between us? I'd have to leave. You know I would.

KENNY   (*Going to her again, more imploringly*)   I kinda go for you, Lila. I guess you know that, don't ya?

LILA   (*More moved than she wants to show*)   Oh, Kenny, you're kidding . . .

KENNY   Ever since the first night you came, the night you . . . put me to bed.

LILA   Kenny, you *did* know. You weren't as drunk as you pretended.

KENNY   (*Smiling*)   Maybe . . . not quite.

LILA   Kenny!

KENNY   It's been kinda hard, living here in the same house with you, Lila. Sleeping in the room right next to you, trying to keep myself from making love to you. Don't you like me a little, Lila? Just a little?

LILA   (*Turning from him, all confusion*)   Kenny, don't ask me.

KENNY   Don't ya?

LILA   I never asked myself that, Kenny. Not once. I haven't dared think of you that way.

KENNY   I . . . I'm lonely, Lila.

LILA   Kenny, you're so young, and so good-lookin'. You could have any girl you wanted.

KENNY   I want *you,* Lila. I can *talk* with you and feel at home with you.

LILA   Kenny, you don't mean those things you're saying. You shouldn't talk like that to a woman if you don't mean it. Things like that excite a woman, so much more'n you know. They raise her hopes, and then, when you don't mean them, those hopes have to fall again. That's happened to me, Kenny. It's happened to me several times. And each time, I think I'm gonna die. I even *pray* to die. Don't tease me, Kenny.

KENNY   (*Beleiving himself completely*)   Lila, I never talked this way to anyone in my life.

LILA   OK. Maybe you do love me. Maybe I love you, too. Maybe I loved you from the first night I arrived, and saw you

77

standing on the porch, just like I used to see your wonderful
daddy. What if we do love each other? We couldn't get
married or . . .

KENNY Why not?

LILA Kenny, you're talking through your hat.

KENNY *Why* am I?

LILA Helen likes me, but she'd never stand for it . . .

KENNY Don't you understand? I'm twenty-one years old. I can
do what I like. Mom's not gonna tell me who to marry. I could
find us a nice little house, all our own, and if Mom din like
it, she wouldn't *have* to.

LILA (*More than her wildest dreams had hoped for*) Kenny.
Stop it. You got me all confused.

KENNY I want a woman like you, Lila. I like it 'cause you're a
little older. What's wrong with a guy marrying a girl a li'l
older than he is? It could be the best thing that happened to
him.

LILA Well, I . . . I dunno, but . . .

KENNY (*Seizing her in his arms again*) Love me, Lila. Love
me.

LILA (*Breathless*) Kenny!

KENNY Mom has to work tonight. She'll be gone. Let's you and
me be together, Lila. Whatta ya say? Please.

78

LILA (*Tearing herself loose*) Kenny, I gotta keep my wits about me. I just know it isn't right, somehow. I just know it wouldn't work. I'm gonna forget all about this. I'm gonna make myself forget everything you've said. I know I'm right, Kenny.

KENNY (*Rejected and sore*) OK. OK.

LILA Kenny, don't be sore.

KENNY If ya wanta turn me down for that . . . that guy with the olive oil on his hair . . .

LILA Kenny, I'm not turning you down. Oh, don't feel that way. I'm just tryin' to do the right thing.

KENNY OK. OK.

LILA Please don't be mad, Kenny. I just can't stand for anyone to be mad at me.

KENNY I'm not mad. Forget it.

LILA Yes you are. I can tell. Oh, sometimes I wish I'd never been born.
     (HELEN *comes in now*)

HELEN Oh, it's good to be home. I wish we could have air-conditioning at the hospital, the same as they do in the movie theatre.
     (*She notices the strain now between* KENNY *and* LILA)

LILA Hi, Helen.

HELEN   Good evening, Lila. Good evening, Kenny. Is dinner about ready?

LILA   Oh, yes. Everything's in the oven.

HELEN   How long have you been home, Son?

KENNY   Just got here.
(HELEN *notices the two glasses* LILA *and* KENNY *have used for cocktails, and the empty beer bottle*)

HELEN   It looks as though the celebrating had already started.

LILA   I made up some cocktails, Helen. I din think you'd mind. A bottle of rum I had. I mixed it with some pineapple juice and put in some cherries. It's awful good. Wanta try it?
(*She pours* HELEN *a glass*)

HELEN   Just a little. I'm going to the revival meeting tonight, before I go back to the hospital. I don't want to shock anyone by having liquor on my breath.

LILA (*Wanting to be a good girl*)   I'll go with you, Helen. I'll go with you to the revival.

HELEN   Oh good! I know it's no use expecting my son to take us.

KENNY   Nope. It's no use.
(HELEN *is still weighing her suspicions*)

HELEN   Kenny, you're usually out of the bath by the time I get home.

KENNY (*Hurrying out of the room*) OK. I'll hurry.
  (HELEN *notices the dining-room table*)

HELEN The table looks lovely, Lila. Where did you get the lovely flowers?

LILA Now don't tell anyone.

HELEN I won't.

LILA Well, I was passing by the school building down the street and no one was around so I picked those out of the big flower bed they've got on the front lawn.

HELEN (*Astounded*) Lila!

LILA Well, no one saw me, Helen. And shoot! the flowers weren't doing anyone any good. School hasn't started yet. And I just couldn't resist them.

HELEN Well, I hope we don't have any angry taxpayers at the door wanting to put you in jail.

LILA Gee, I hope I haven't disgraced you, Helen.

HELEN . . . As long as no one saw you, what the taxpayers don't know won't hurt them.

LILA Will Kenny sit at the table where his father would be?

HELEN Uh . . . no, Lila. I'll sit at the head.

LILA Oh! (LILA *thinks about this for a moment*) Do you always celebrate your anniversaries this way?

HELEN Yes. Ever since the dinner you attended back in Oklahoma when you were a girl. It's still the anniversary of my marriage, even though Kenneth is gone. It's one of the few things in the world I have to celebrate, so I go right on. Before Kenny graduated, I used to ask one or two of his teachers. And sometimes I have the minister and his wife. Maybe I *should* let Kenny sit at the head of the table, but . . . (*Finds a reason to justify herself*) But he never learned to carve.

LILA I'll go take another look at the chicken.
(*She goes into the kitchen*)

HELEN Any word from Ricky yet, Lila?

LILA No, Helen. I'm beginning to get discouraged.

HELEN How long has it been now? Four weeks?

LILA (*Returning from the kitchen*) Yah. Four weeks. And I haven't heard a thing.

HELEN Well, it may take another four weeks, with times as bad as they are.

LILA Oh, I hope not. (*Sits*) I'm getting so depressed, being out of work and everything. I get awfully depressed when I'm not working, Helen.

HELEN You mustn't let yourself.

LILA Oh, I try to keep from it, but I just can't seem to help it. The doctor up in North Dakota told me I should *keep* working. He said to always keep busy doing *something,* no matter what, just to keep my mind off *myself.*

82

HELEN   Maybe you should try to make other friends, besides Kenny and me. Why don't you call on Mrs. Mulvaney sometime? She's about your age and I know you'd like her.

LILA   I'm awful shy about meeting new people, Helen. Nice married women like her, who have kids and go to church and seem so happy . . . I just don't seem to have anything in common with.

HELEN   You'd get over those feelings. And maybe you could get yourself a job here in town.

LILA   Helen, what could *I* do?

HELEN   You could get a job in one of the stores, maybe. Pretty as you are, you'd draw customers.

LILA   Jobs like that are scarce.

HELEN   But you could look.

LILA   You're getting tired of me, aren't you, Helen?

HELEN   I didn't say that, Lila.

LILA   Helen, I'd be just scared to death to take a job in one of those stores downtown. I just don't have confidence in myself to do things like that. I couldn't even wrap up a paper of pins without trembling.

HELEN   Really, Lila?

LILA   Honest, Helen. I get so scared I get sick.

HELEN But you've enough confidence to get out onstage and perform for people.

LILA That's different, Helen. I can't tell you why, but it's different.

HELEN Well, we won't talk about it any more. Forget it. You're being a big help to me taking care of the house.

LILA That's about the only kinda work I can do, except in shows.

HELEN You can stay on for a while just as you are, just as long as Kenny doesn't mind . . .

LILA I've tried to get him to take back his room, Helen. But he just won't listen.

HELEN You should feel honored. Kenny isn't usually so generous. I guess he's willing to give up his room in order to get home cooking.

LILA You taught me all the cooking I know, Helen.

HELEN But I'm out of practice now. I've given up the art. It just makes Kenny more dependent on me. Was the chicken done?

LILA Yah. I turned out the fire and left it in the oven to keep warm till Kenny's ready.

HELEN Sometimes he takes longer in the bathroom than a girl. My, that drink was refreshing.

LILA Want some more?

HELEN No. No more.

LILA I gave Kenny a drink, Helen. Was that all right?

HELEN As long as he drinks anyway, it's just as well for him to do it at home, I suppose, in a sociable way. Besides, he insists on keeping *beer* in the icebox. Oh yes, he's very grown up. (*A little suspiciously*) How long was he here before I got home, Lila?

LILA Oh, fifteen minutes, maybe. I dunno.

HELEN (*She may sound a little envious*) Were you dancing together?

LILA Yah . . . just kiddin' around.

HELEN The two of you are here alone together quite often, aren't you?

LILA Oh, not often, Helen. Usually when he's here, I'm straightening up the house or washing out his socks or fixing him something to eat.

HELEN You're just what he's been waiting for. Another mother to pamper him.

LILA I *love* to do things for him, Helen.

HELEN All right, but I'm warning you. He can make himself very appealing. I hope he behaves himself when he's with you.

85

LILA Oh sure, Helen. You don't have to worry about anything like that. (*Wanting to change the subject*) Can you keep a secret, Helen? He's brought you a present.

HELEN Oh, no!

LILA I know what it is but I can't tell.

HELEN Oh, I hope he hasn't gone and wasted his money on something foolish.

LILA Shucks, if he wants to bring you a present, why not?

HELEN It doesn't seem right.

LILA Helen . . . I know he didn't swipe it, if that's what's bothering you. He showed me the receipt, bought and paid for.

HELEN I wasn't thinking of that.

LILA Paid a plenty for, too. He told me he's been saving for it all summer.

HELEN That's why he couldn't make the down payment on the car. I can't take it.

LILA But, Helen, he'd feel terrible if you didn't.

HELEN I'm his mother. I don't want him to waste his gifts on *me*.

LILA But you can't refuse it, Helen. You can't refuse a man's gift. Do you know something? Sometimes it's more blessed

86

Warren Beatty, Carol Haney, and Betty Field,
as KENNY, LILA, and HELEN

to receive than it is to give. I remember a preacher saying that once when I was a little girl.

KENNY (*From the bathroom*)   Dinner ready?

LILA (*Calling back*)   I'm putting it on right now, Kenny.
(*She runs into kitchen as* KENNY *comes out, all cleaned up, wearing a new pair of slacks and a pair of white shoes.* HELEN *looks at him astounded*)

HELEN   Well! look at our fashion plate.

LILA (*Bringing in the dishes from the kitchen*)   My, you look handsome, Kenny.

KENNY (*Embarrassed to be complimented*)   Well . . . I just thought I'd clean up a little. (*He goes to the table in the living room, opens a drawer and brings out the present for his mother*) Present for you, Mom.

HELEN   Oh now, Kenny, you shouldn't have.

LILA   Go on and open it, Helen.

HELEN   I . . . I can't.

KENNY   For cryin' out loud! I bring you a present and you're not even gonna open it.

HELEN   I just hope you haven't gone and done anything foolish.

LILA   Helen, open it. Go on.
(*Reluctantly,* HELEN *opens the package.* KENNY *looks on expectantly*)

HELEN Well, I . . .

LILA When young men bring *me* presents, you sure don't see *me* hesitate.

HELEN (*The package opened, she finds a lovely watch in the box*) Kenny! A watch!
   (*A smile of pride comes over his face.* LILA *rushes to see the present*)

LILA Oh, isn't it lovely!

KENNY (*Waiting for* HELEN *to respond*) It's twenty-two jewels, Mom. Lifetime guarantee. You can throw your old watch away.

HELEN (*Her face begins to twist in an effort to keep from crying*) Kenny, I . . . I . . . (*But she can say nothing. She jumps up and runs to the kitchen*)

KENNY (*Puzzled*) What's wrong with her?

LILA You just wait. She's just trying to get her feelings under control. She'll be back to say thank you.

KENNY I give up. I never know how she's gonna act.
   (HELEN *returns now, a look of deep misgiving on her face, the present in her hand*)

HELEN I . . . can't take it, Kenny.

KENNY (*Thunderstruck*) Huh?

HELEN I just can't take it. I appreciate your intentions, but it's too nice, Kenny. A watch like this must have cost you fifty dollars. I can't let you do it for me. I'll keep the watch your father gave me. I can have it fixed.

KENNY (*Intensely angry*) It's *my* business what I give, and *my* business what it costs me.

HELEN Take it back to the jeweler, Kenny, and get your money back. Get me some *little* present if you want to, something for the house, maybe, that doesn't cost much.
(LILA *sees that* KENNY's *hurt is putting him into a deep rage—his face beginning to whiten, his body stiffening*)

LILA She doesn't mean it, Kenny. She wants the present. Really she does. You've changed your mind, haven't you, Helen? You're going to take the present, aren't you?

HELEN (*Falling into a chair*) I . . . I can't.

KENNY (*Having come to an inner decision*) OK! (*He stalks to the living room*) I'm moving outa here. You'll find me from now on, over at Jelly's house.

HELEN (*Jumping up*) Kenny, you can't leave now. We've got this lovely dinner waiting to feed you. Now come back here and sit down and quit being silly.

LILA (*Feeling for him intensely*) Oh, Kenny!

KENNY (*In a full and frightening blast*) I don't want any lovely dinners. I'm sick of women tending me and looking after me. Your *lovely* dinner would fall into my stomach like garbage.

89

Go on and feed your lovely dinners to yourselves. I'm gettin' out.

(He stalks to the door)

LILA *(Running after him)* Kenny, Helen doesn't mean it. Come back, Kenny. She wants your present.

KENNY She can go to hell and find out what time it is down there.

(He goes out, letting the screen door slam behind him. HELEN huddles in a chair, convulsed in tears)

HELEN Oh, my boy! What have I done to hurt him?

LILA Why didn't you take the present, Helen?

HELEN I couldn't.

LILA But why?

HELEN Something just rose inside me and forced me to refuse.

LILA He just wanted to make up for his father's being gone. He just wanted to do what big Kenneth would have done.

HELEN I can't let him do the things his father did, Lila.

LILA But every boy wants to be like his father.

HELEN There are some ways he can't be allowed.

LILA But a *present* . . . that he wanted to *give* you.

HELEN I couldn't take it.

LILA   You can be hard, Helen.

HELEN   Yes. When I have to be.

LILA   I could never be hard that way.

HELEN   We pay for our weaknesses.

LILA   Yes. You have to be hard to be good, don't you? People aren't really sinful, are they, Helen? They're just weak and soft . . . like me. (*Her face holds a sad admission of defeat. She looks at the deserted dining-room table*) This lovely dinner going to waste.

HELEN   I couldn't eat a thing.

LILA (*With a pang*)   Oh, I can't bear to see lovely things go to waste.

HELEN   I'm going to get ready for the revival.
   (*In the background now, we hear the organ music, a soft hymn being played; people pass the house in pairs on their way to the tent, the women all carrying palm leaf fans, the men looking uncomfortably serious.* HELEN *exits into her room. The telephone rings.* LILA *answers it*)

LILA   Hello? . . . (*She recognizes the voice and exclaims joyfully*) Ricky! Oh gee! it's good to hear you. (*Pause*) You're here in town? (*She listens*) You've got a job? Oh, Ricky! I can't believe it. (*Listens*) Yah. I'll be here. I'll be waiting for you on the front porch. I can't wait. Hurry. (*She hangs up and calls back to* HELEN) Helen! Guess what. It's Ricky! He's got me a job. A wonderful job. A hundred dollars a week.

He's taking me back with him tomorrow. Did you hear me, Helen?

HELEN (*From her room*) That's splendid, Lila.

LILA (*Dancing about the room in joy*) Oh, I can't believe it. A hundred bucks a week. Sometimes more, he said. Oh, I'm so happy I could cry.

HELEN (*Coming from her room now, ready to leave*) Then I take it, you won't be going to the revival.

LILA No, Helen. I gotta wait for Ricky. Oh, I'm so thrilled. Just think. A job! A hundred dollars a week, in times like these.

HELEN With a show?

LILA Well, I s'pose. He din say exactly. He said he'd tell me all about it when he got here.

HELEN I'm very happy for you, Lila.

LILA Thanks, Helen. Oh, I'm so excited, I don't know what to do.

HELEN (*Starting for the door*) Well, I'll see you in the morning.

LILA Oh, I'll be in early tonight. Rick's just gonna take me for a ride. I won't stay out late.

HELEN Oh! Well, I thought . . . (*She hesitates out of discretion*) . . . nothing.

LILA What? What'd you think, Helen?

HELEN (*Gently*) I thought maybe you'd want to spend the night with Ricky somewhere.
(LILA *blushes*)

LILA Helen!

HELEN I'm not a prude, Lila. I may be religious but I'm not a prude. I know your life has been different from mine. A beautiful girl like you, out with a show. I knew Ricky was your lover the minute I saw him. I don't sit in judgment on people.

LILA I supposed you'd think I was terrible if you knew.

HELEN No, dear. Now you and Ricky be together. I know you want to be.

LILA You're just wonderful, Helen.

HELEN If Kenny comes back, we'll think up some explanation for him, though I don't know why we should bother. He probably knows more now than the two of us put together. Oh, I hate to see young people so precocious about these matters.

LILA That organ music's pretty, isn't it? And the choir sounds so sweet and holy.

HELEN Yes. This is the first year I've gone to the revival meetings, and I'm getting a lot out of them.

LILA (*In a mood for repentance*) Helen . . . I hope you don't think I'm too terrible, me and Rick.

HELEN   I know I'm *fond* of you, Lila. I just don't think about these personal things.

LILA   I've always wanted to tell somebody, Helen, how bad I feel . . . how much I regret . . . all the silly things I've done in my life.

HELEN   (*Anticipating a confession*)   No, now. Regret is foolish. Let the past be gone. You just bring it back again with regrets.

LILA   I've always wanted to be good, Helen. Deep in my heart, I've always felt I *was* good. And the things that've happened in the past, some of 'em, don't fit, and it makes me feel ugly and humiliated to remember them.

HELEN   Now, Lila, you've no need to confess to *me*.

LILA   But I want to, Helen. Now that I've got this new job and feel so good about everything, I feel I can atone to somebody. You're the only person who can hear me.

HELEN   All right.

LILA   I . . . I've done lots of awful crazy things in my life that were perfectly terrible.

HELEN   Now you've said it.

LILA   I'm weak, Helen. The doctor told me I was emotionally immature. And I know what he meant, because sometimes I feel like a child, just as helpless as a child, and as afraid as a child. And when I get afraid, that's when I do silly things.

94

When I'm afraid, I want somebody close to me, Helen. I don't care who it is, but I've gotta have someone close. Sometimes men take advantage of this. And that's when I do the things I regret. That's when I hate myself.

HELEN Well, you've got a brand-new job now, and you can start all over again. And forget these memories.

LILA (*Smiling, relieved of her guilt*) Yah. I will, Helen. I feel lots better about things now.
(*Organ music is heard in the background*)

HELEN We all have to get things off our chests sometimes. Oh, they're playing the opening music now. I must hurry.

LILA See you in the morning, Helen.

HELEN If Kenny comes back, tell him I'm sorry. Tell him I'll take the watch, if he really wants me to have it.
(HELEN *starts for the door*)

LILA Oh, I'm glad, Helen.

HELEN Good night, Lila.

LILA G'night.
(HELEN *gone*, LILA *takes the dishes from the table out to the kitchen and puts them away, while, in the background, we hear the voice of the* EVANGELIST. *When she finishes clearing the table,* LILA *comes out onto the door-step, lights a cigarette, sits and waits*)

VOICE OF THE EVANGELIST It is very heartening to see so many of you congregated here tonight, in the midst of these troubling times. Yes, the Depression! We hear a lot of talk these days about the Depression, don't we, friends? And all through this great country of ours, we know there are millions of hungry men and women and children, walking through the streets of our great cities, searching vainly for work, waiting in line for food, trying to fight off starvation and despair. And I have heard, all over this great country, the cries of helpless people saying, "What am I to do?" and I feel for them in their plight, these countless people all over our land today who are asking themselves and their brothers, "What am I to do? How am I to live?"

(*The* EVANGELIST *pauses here. We hear* RICKY'S *car drive up at the left.* LILA *cries out and runs off to greet him*)

LILA Ricky!

VOICE OF THE EVANGELIST And as I was on my way to your town, traveling by bus over the once great farm lands of our country, I saw the tragic faces of our farmers who have been battling the Depression and the Drought. With haunted faces, they would turn to me and say, "My land is ruined. My soil is destroyed. Things will no longer grow. My cattle are starving and dying of thirst, and they drop to the ground in the parching sun, and I can do nothing to save them. What am I to do? How am I to live?" (RICKY *and* LILA *come on arm in arm, billing and cooing and petting*) And then there is that other kind of Depression, friends. The depression of the heart, the drought of the soul, the deflation of the spirit. And this is the worst Depression of all. For the heart closes its doors like a bank vault when people are afraid to give of their love, and there is a sorrow all over the land when there is not enough love to go around, and hopeless faces look at you pleadingly and cry out in despair, "How am I to live? How am I to live?" Yes. That is the question all of us are asking ourselves today, friends. What am I to do? How *am* I . . . to live? (*A pause*) Let us pray.

> (LILA *and* RICKY *have been mumbling to each other since their entrance together, during the* EVANGELIST'S *speech*)

RICKY   Miss me?

LILA   Oh, Daddy, you know I did.

RICKY   Been a good girl while Daddy's been gone?

LILA   Yes. I really have, Daddy. I go to bed every night at ten-thirty and get up in the morning at seven. Oh, I been so good. You wouldn't believe it.

RICKY   I'll change all that now. You need a li'l fun, don't ya, baby?

LILA   (*Laughing softly*)   Yah. I do, Daddy. I need a good time.

RICKY   I'm here to give it to ya.
> (*They kiss again. The* EVANGELIST'S *speech has ended and we now hear the mumbling voices of the congregation in prayer*)

LILA   Tell me about the job, Rick.

RICKY   Relax. I got a bottle a gin out in the car and a couple of reefers. Let's have a li'l ride first. Whatta ya say? And we'll have a few drinks and . . .

97

LILA   Oh, Ricky, I'm too anxious. I wanta hear about it now. Tell me.

RICKY   Don't be so curious, baby. Just follow along with me. I wouldn't steer ya wrong, would I?

LILA   But what kind of a job *is* it? Where do we work? Whatta we do?

RICKY   Gimme time, baby. I'll tell ya everything. Let's get tanked up first. Whatta ya say?

LILA   I'm not going one step until you tell me about the job.

RICKY   What are ya worried about? It's a swell job, I tell ya. Who ever offered ya a hundred bucks a week before?

LILA   I'm thrilled, Rick. But I wanta know what we do, and where we play.

RICKY   Well . . . there's a couple a places, roadhouses, on the outskirts of Kaycee.

LILA   Oh! Whatta we do, Rick? Do I sing and dance?

RICKY   Well, maybe. We make a few movies, too.

LILA   Movies? Rick, they don't make movies in Kanz City, do they?

RICKY   Yah. Sure. Oh, it's not on a very big scale. But they pay. Sometimes we'll make a lot more'n a hundred a week. There's convention dates to play, too.

LILA (*Showing her first suspicion*) Conventions?

RICKY Yah. In the fall.

LILA Rick . . . whatta we do at . . . conventions?

RICKY Now, look, baby, it's nothin' you and me haven't done before, except that . . .

LILA (*Frightened*) Rick, what kind of a job *is* it? *Tell* me!

RICKY Now don't go hysterical on me. I'm tellin' you, it's nothin' you and me haven't done before, and ya don't have to let another guy touch ya. And when you make the movies, you can wear a mask, if you want to.

LILA (*Screaming*) Rick!

RICKY Keep your voice down, Lila.

LILA Rick, it's blue movies you're talking about, isn't it? Yah. And a sex act. That's what we do in the roadhouse, isn't it?

RICKY Look, after you've done it a few times, you won't have any squeamish feelings about it at all.

LILA No. After I done it a few times, I don't suppose I'd have any feelings about anything.

RICKY I been lookin' all over the town for jobs. Not even a carnival is booking outa there now. It's the only job I been able to find. The town is wide-open now. They got things goin' on there now ya couldn't see in New Orleans. It's the only money there is, I'm *telling* you.

99

LILA   I don't want any of it. Get outa here, Rick.

RICKY   Look, baby, think twice before throwing away dough like that.

LILA   I'd starve before I did it. I'd starve.

RICKY   Yah? Did ya ever *try* starving? *I* have.

LILA   I'm willing to try.

RICKY   OK. But not me.

LILA   Then go on and do it. Go on and do it. But don't come near me again.

RICKY   I got no job without you.

LILA   Why?

RICKY   The whole world's crazy for a pair of big ones like you got. (*He points to her breasts*) That's what they want.

LILA   (*Hiding her breasts*)   You make me ashamed.

RICKY   (*Seizing her by the wrist, twisting until she winces with pain*)   You're coming with me in this.

LILA   (*Slapping him with her other hand*)   Let me go!

RICKY   (*Fuming*)   OK, baby. Get tough with me and see where it'll getcha.

LILA   I'll get as tough with you as I like. I don't have to depend on you no more. I got very respectable friends here who'll protect me.

RICKY   Oh yeah?

LILA   Yeah! So put that in your pipe and smoke it.
(JELLY *and* KENNY *appear at the corner down left.* LILA *and* RICKY *become stiff and silent upon seeing the two boys*)

KENNY   You go on home then and tell your old lady I'm moving in.

JELLY   OK, Ken! For three bucks a week she'll let ya have the whole house.

KENNY   I'll be over soon as I get some clothes packed.
(JELLY *runs off and* KENNY *comes on, merely recognizing* LILA *and* RICKY *with a muted "Hi" as he passes them and goes into the house.* RICKY *returns the "Hi."* LILA *is a little more cognizant*)

LILA   Hello, Kenny.
(*Inside the house,* KENNY *gets out an old suitcase and begins to stuff his clothes into it.* RICKY *speaks now, keeping his voice lowered*)

RICKY   Maybe your friends here'd like to see some a the pictures ya posed for that time up in Grand Rapids.

LILA   Ricky! you wouldn't do a thing like that.

RICKY   They might like to see 'em.

LILA I was drunk when that happened. And I didn't know you had a camera.

RICKY I still got the pictures.

LILA You ornery son of a bitch!

RICKY I get along, baby.

LILA Go on and show your pictures. I don't care. I'm not scared of you, Rick. I got plenty on *you,* too. I can make just as much trouble for you as you can for me. And I'll do it, too. Don't think I won't.

RICKY I'm not goin' without *you.* (*He grabs her by the wrist*) Now go in there and pack your clothes. We'll spend the night at the tourist camp and go to Kaycee in the morning. Go on, God damn it, before I knock your teeth out.

LILA (*Screaming wildly*) Help me, someone! Help me, Kenny!
     (RICKY *had not expected her to call* KENNY. *He drops her wrist*)

RICKY God damn you!
     (KENNY *comes running to the porch*)

KENNY Whatsa trouble, Lila?

LILA You better go now, Rick.
     (RICKY *looks at* KENNY *contemptuously*)

RICKY OK, leading man! Take over.
     (*Knowing he is foiled, he quickly vanishes.* LILA *runs to* KENNY'S *arms*)

LILA   Oh, Kenny!

KENNY   Whatsa matter, Lila? What'd he do?
        (*He acts as though he would start out for* RICKY *to beat him up*)

LILA   Let him go, Kenny! Don't pay any attention to him. Just let him go.

KENNY   Did he hurt you or anything, Lila?

LILA   No. I'm all right. (*She clings to* KENNY) Just hold me, Kenny.
       (*She is sobbing almost hysterically*)

KENNY   (*Comfortingly*)   Sure, Lila. (*Slowly aware of her*) Gee, Lila, you're trembling.

LILA   I know. If you just hold me close for a few minutes, I'll be all right.

KENNY   Sure, Lila. (*He stands holding her in his arms, smoothing his hands over her shoulder consolingly*) Are you better now, Lila?

LILA   (*Very softly, almost mouselike*)   Yes, Kenny. Oh, a man's arms can be so strong and helpful. Did you know that, Kenny?

KENNY   Can they, Lila?

LILA   Oh yes. They can be strong and helpful, or they can be strong and harmful, either one.

KENNY   I . . . wanna be *helpful,* Lila.

LILA Do ya, Kenny?

KENNY Yes. I do. Relax, Lila. No one's gonna hurt you.

LILA (*Still in his arms*) Sometimes I wish I could crawl inside a man's big roomy chest and just live there, warm and protected.

KENNY (*Touched, moved by her*) Lila!

LILA Did you mean those things you said earlier tonight, Kenny?

KENNY Sure, Lila. I could hold you like this forever, Lila.

LILA Kenny!
    (*She lifts her head and he kisses her*)

KENNY I'll take care of you, Lila. I'll take care of you.
    (*All we hear from* LILA *is a long sigh of crying relief*)

Curtain

Scene Two

It is a little after seven o'clock the next morning. KENNY *still lies in bed—in* LILA'S *bed—trying to prolong the night's sleep.* LILA *herself is out in the kitchen getting breakfast. She is radiantly happy again, singing to herself as she prepares the food. Then she comes to the bedroom, in her nightrobe and slippers, and rouses* KENNY.

LILA   Kenny! (*He mumbles protests*) Kenny, hurry up and get ready for breakfast. Your mother will be back any minute now, Kenny. And I've got to get things straightened up before she gets here. Now get up. Please.

KENNY (*Lifting himself to a sitting position*)   OK. Get me my robe, will ya, Lila?

LILA   Yes. (*She brings him his robe. He doesn't bother with slippers*) Now, hurry, Kenny. I'll get everything straightened up so Helen won't suspect.

KENNY (*Half-conscious, starting to the bathroom*)   Yah . . .

LILA   Your breakfast is on the table. I'll get the bed made up now.
       (*She makes up the bed as* JELLY *comes to the front door*)

JELLY   Kenny here?

(handwritten note in top margin) when a mother

LILA   He's washing, Jelly. Then he's got to eat his breakfast.

JELLY (*Coming in*)   Where'd he go last night?

LILA (*A little troubled*)   Uh . . . I dunno.

JELLY   He said he was coming over to my house. My mom got the room all ready for him. She put clean sheets on the bed an' everything. And he never showed up.

LILA (*Troubled, confused*)   Oh, well, I don't know anything about that, Jelly. You'll have to ask Kenny when you see him.

JELLY   It sure is funny, Ken sayin' he was comin' over to my house and then not showin' up.

LILA   I dunno anything about it, Jelly.

JELLY   I'm not a moocher or anything, but I think Ken owes me a cigarette for the trouble he caused my mom, and everything.

LILA (*Offering her own pack*)   Here's a cigarette.

JELLY   Thanks. (*Suddenly he gets a little more courage*) Oh . . . ya spose I could have another one for later?

LILA (*Coming through*)   Here.

JELLY (*Lighting up*)   Thanks. Tell Ken I'll see him later. (JELLY *runs off*) LILA *finishes the bed and goes to the kitchen as* KENNY *comes from the bathroom, dressed in a fresh uniform, his hair combed, his face scrubbed. But there is a dirty look on his face, the expression of a man who is troubled by his conscience)*

KENNY Was that Jelly?

LILA Yah. He said his mother got a room ready for you last night.

KENNY Oh, I forgot.
(*He sits at the kitchen table and begins eating*)

LILA You shoulda called him last night, Kenny.

KENNY They don't have a telephone.

LILA Oh. Well, I guess it doesn't matter. But it looks like we're going to be blackmailed for cigarettes for a while.

KENNY Don't worry. I can take care a him.

LILA I'm not gonna worry about anything this morning, Kenny. (*She sits on his lap and kisses him*) I'm too happy. God, I'm happy. I'm the kinda person who goes around feeling miserable for so long that I forget what it's like to be happy. I forget happiness even exists. Then something happens that just blows all the dark clouds away, and I see the sun shining again, and I have a good feeling in my heart that makes me glad I'm alive and want to live forever. (*She kisses him again. He is not very responsive*) Aren't you happy, Kenny?

KENNY (*Not convincingly*) Yah . . . sure. I'm happy.

LILA Oh, you're young. You still take a day of happiness for granted. I don't. But I don't know that I ever could. (*Notices that* KENNY *has eaten very little and is now lighting his after-breakfast cigarette*) Whatsa matter, Kenny? You din eat much breakfast.

KENNY   Nothin'.

LILA   Didn't I fix your eggs right?

KENNY   They're OK.

LILA   What is it, Kenny?

KENNY   I . . . kept having bad dreams last night.

LILA   Ya did?

KENNY   Yah. Awful dreams. I don't understand.

LILA   What about?

KENNY   (*Feeling guilt, being evasive*)   I dunno.

LILA   Tell me, Kenny.

KENNY   I . . . I dreamed that someone died.

LILA   Who?

KENNY   It was . . . Mom.

LILA   Oh!

KENNY   We were both in a big cave together, all dark and

damp, and I found a way out but I couldn't take her. She had to die if I was going to live. She had to die, for some reason. She had to. It was terrible.

LILA   It was only a dream, Kenny.

KENNY   But it seemed so real.

LILA   Kenny, dreams usually mean the opposite of what they are. Do you know that? When you dream of a death, it's supposed to mean . . . a wedding. Did you know that, Kenny? (KENNY *swallows hard. There is a silence*) You know, Kenny, I've been thinking about it since I got up, and I think maybe Helen wouldn't mind at all if we got married. Helen might think it was the best thing in the world. (*The mention of marriage now disturbs* KENNY) Oh, Kenny! I can be so true to a man. I can be so loving and helpful if a man'll just let me. Oh, I'm going to make you happy, Kenny. I'll make you the happiest man . . .

KENNY   (*Interrupting her*)   Lila!
       (*She stops and looks at him*)

LILA   Yes, Kenny?

KENNY   Lila, I din say for *sure* we'd get married, did I? (LILA *freezes, without moving or speaking*) Look here, Lila, I wanta do the right thing, and all that, but . . . I din really *promise* anything, did I? (*He waits for an answer*) Did I?

LILA   (*Total defeat in her voice*)   No, Kenny.

KENNY   . . . And after all, Lila, you *are* a little older'n me . . .

just a little. That's bound to make a difference, Lila, when you come right down to it.

LILA (*Lifeless*) Yah.

KENNY Ya know, Lila, you may have been right in the first place, when you were telling me yesterday that things wouldn't work out for us. I see that now. You . . . may have been right from the very beginning.
(*This is the blow she had feared. The life has gone out of her like the air from a bladder*)

LILA And ya din really mean any a the things ya said.

KENNY Well . . . I meant 'em in a way, Lila. I mean, I thought I did. That is, I do like you, Lila.

LILA . . . Thanks.

KENNY It's just that I feel so darn much different now . . .

LILA Now that ya got what ya wanted.

KENNY Gee, Lila, I don't see why ya have to put it that way. I'm tellin' ya, I do like you an awful lot. It's just that, I realize now it wouldn't be right for us to be married.

LILA Forget it, Kenny.

KENNY Look, Lila, it's like I wanted something my whole life that now I don't want any more. It's like I was seeing something in an entirely new way. Can ya understand, Lila?

LILA Sure, Kenny.

KENNY Do ya, Lila?

LILA Sure. I gotta be getting dressed now, Kenny.

KENNY Oh yah. Sure, Lila.
(KENNY *returns to living room.* LILA *shuts the door between them and hurries into the hallway to the bathroom.* KENNY *sits on the davenport in a deep funk.* HELEN
now comes onto the porch and into the house)

HELEN Good morning.

KENNY (*Lifelessly*) Hi, Mom!

HELEN I just saw Mrs. Beamis. She said you didn't go over
there last night.

KENNY Nope.

HELEN Well . . . who made your bed this morning?

KENNY (*Rising, angrily*) A band of little fairies flew right in
through the window and presto! There it was. All ready for
the *Good Housekeeping* Seal of Approval.

HELEN (*Sensing his mood*) What's the matter with you?

KENNY (*Getting to his feet and starting for the door*) Nothin'.
I'm goin' to work.
(*Now we hear* LILA *sobbing in the bathroom. The sobs
are those of a desperately frightened child*)

HELEN (*Alarmed*) What's that?

KENNY I dunno.

HELEN Is Lila here? (KENNY *nods*) I thought she went off with Ricky last night. When did she get back?

KENNY (*Choking with guilt*) Uh . . . I . . .

HELEN (*In full voice*) Did you and Lila spend the night here together? (*No answer*) Did you?
> (LILA *now bursts out of the bathroom, making* KENNY's *answer unnecessary. She holds one wrist with her other hand, and blood covers her arm. She is screaming hysterically*)

LILA Helen! Help me! I don't wanta die. I don't wanta die. Not really. Help me, Helen!

HELEN (*Jumping back into duty*) My God! (*She grabs* LILA, *forces her onto the bed and looks at the wrist*) What in God's name have you done here, Lila? (HELEN *is in full command now, of herself and of the situation*) Kenny, get me my first-aid. Right away.

KENNY (*Alert now*) Yah.
> (*He runs back to* HELEN's *room.* LILA *is sobbing tragically*)

HELEN (*Inspecting the wound*) What'd you use?

LILA Kenny's razor.

HELEN It's all right. You didn't get to the vein. You're not going to die.

LILA I never saw so much blood.

HELEN It's all right. You didn't cut the vein. I'll get the bleed-ing stopped as soon as I get your wrist taped. (KENNY *returns with the first-aid kit*) Tear off some strips of gauze for me, Son.

KENNY (*Terrified*) Yah.
   (HELEN *paints the wound with mercurochrome*)

HELEN This'll prevent any infection. (KENNY *hands her the gauze and she binds* LILA's *wrist*) Now cut some tape for me.

KENNY Yah.

HELEN (*Winding the gauze around* LILA's *wrist*) You haven't done yourself any serious harm, Lila. You'll be good as new as soon as I get the bandages on. Bring me a glass of water, Kenny.
   (KENNY *runs to the kitchen*)

LILA (*Still sobbing hysterically*) I don't know what made me do it, Helen. Honest, I don't. You won't have to report me, will you?

HELEN I'm supposed to, Lila. I could get into serious trouble if this were discovered.

LILA Oh, Helen, if they found out, they might make me go back to another of those hospitals. I don't want to, Helen. Please don't report it.

HELEN All right. I'll take a chance. What are you going to do, Lila?

LILA I don't know, Helen.

HELEN Well, you can stay here and rest a few days if you feel you should, but . . .

LILA I better go, Helen.

HELEN Is Ricky still here?

LILA Yah.

HELEN Do you feel like going with him?

LILA I guess so.
     (KENNY *returns with a glass of water, giving it to* HELEN)

HELEN Take this pill, Lila. It'll calm you.
     (LILA *swallows the pill with water*)

LILA Call Ricky for me, will you, Helen? He's out at the tourist camp. Tell him I'll be ready by the time he gets here.

HELEN Are you sure you feel like it?

LILA Yah. I'm sure.

HELEN All right. I'll call him. But you'd better rest until he gets here.
     (HELEN *goes to telephone and calls.* KENNY *stands inside* LILA's *door and just looks at her, frightened and awed*)

KENNY (*In a soft voice*) Lila!

LILA See there? You never knew your Aunt Lila was such a silly girl, did you, Kenny?

KENNY Lila, you're not gonna go away with that guy Ricky, are ya?

LILA Yes, Kenny!

KENNY Lila, that guy's no good. You can tell it just by lookin' at him.

LILA Now, Kenny!

KENNY And you were havin' a fight last night. He was gonna hit you.

LILA We'll get along all right, him and me, from now on. You don't have to worry, Kenny.

KENNY Lila, I been thinkin' it all over. It might not be such a bad idea, you and me getting married. I mean . . .

LILA Forget it, Kenny.

KENNY I'm serious, Lila. If you really want to, I'll go tell Mom right now that that's what we're gonna do . . .

LILA I got no strings on you, Kenny. I got no strings on anyone. You can forget you ever knew me.

KENNY I never can, Lila.

LILA Yes you can. You're a man. Men can forget almost anything, in time. In another few months, you'll forget you ever knew me.

KENNY Lila!

(*He turns now, close to tears, and comes into living
room.* HELEN *returns from making her call to* RICKY)

HELEN Close her door and let her rest. I gave her a little seda-
tive to hold her steady. I want it to take effect. (KENNY *closes
the door as* LILA *rests peacefully on the bed.* HELEN *and* KENNY
now face each other, KENNY's *face full of guilt and misgiving*)
What happened?

KENNY Whatta ya mean?

HELEN I mean exactly what I say. What happened?

KENNY Well, I . . . I . . .

HELEN You made love to her, didn't you?

KENNY . . . Yes.

HELEN I've been expecting something like this. Was this the
first time?

KENNY Yes.

HELEN Dear God! What kind of a son have I? A woman old
enough to be your mother.

KENNY No she isn't.

HELEN Almost. What caused her to do this? Did you abuse
her in some way? Did you mistreat her?

KENNY (*Suddenly bawling*)   What do you think I am? Some kind of a brute, or something? What do you think I *am?*

HELEN (*Quietly*)   I . . . don't know, Kenny. All I know is, a woman doesn't try to kill herself when a man just . . . just makes love to her.

KENNY   I . . . I told her . . . we might get married.

HELEN   Dear God! And she believed you.

KENNY   I . . . I thought I meant it. Then . . . I woke up this morning, and . . . I felt different somehow. I . . . I couldn't.

HELEN   Lila! A guest here in our own house. Someone as close to us as kin. And you couldn't leave her alone. You had to prove your manliness, didn't you?

KENNY   Oh, lay off, Mom! For Christ sake, lay off!

HELEN   You did it to spite me, didn't you?

KENNY   I tell you, I thought I loved her.

HELEN   You did it to spite *me.*

KENNY (*Suddenly rising to meet her accusation*)   Well, I don't mind letting you know that *some*one can love me.

HELEN (*With sudden shock*)   Oh! (KENNY *can't look at her*) And you've always thought I didn't.

KENNY (*Starts for the door evasively*)   I gotta be goin' to work.

HELEN (*Running to him, grasping his sleeve*) Kenny, come back here.

KENNY I gotta go, Mom. I'll be late.

HELEN What have you expected of me all these years, Kenny? Tell me.

KENNY (*Pulling away, still unable to face her*) Let me go, Mom.

HELEN (*Demanding*) *Tell* me, Kenny. Tell me.

KENNY (*Cornered, he turns and faces her*) I don't expect *any-thing* of you any more. You never gave a damn about me. You gotta be so gol-darned independent, and to show the whole world you can take care of yourself. Well, power to ya!

HELEN Kenny!

KENNY Yes, I did it to spite you. Every crazy thing I ever did in my whole life, I did to spite you.

HELEN Oh, Kenny, all these years you've thought I neglected you.

KENNY Dad was the only man in this family you ever loved. Oh sure, *he* was the hero of this family. Not me.

HELEN Kenny, let your father rest in peace.

KENNY I'm sorry.

HELEN   I've loved you as much as I dared, Son.

KENNY   Oh, sure!

HELEN   If I'd loved you any more, I'd have destroyed you.
(*Stifling her tears,* HELEN *runs back to her room, leaving* KENNY *with a feeling of shock and despair*)

KENNY   Mom!
(HELEN *is gone.* KENNY *throws himself down on the sofa and sobs. Then he rises and begins to think. Slowly, he goes to the table and takes the jeweler's box with the watch out of the drawer. Then solemnly, as though performing a mysterious rite, he goes to* LILA's *door and taps softly*)

LILA   (*In a weak voice*)   Come in.

KENNY   (*Entering*)   It's me, Lila.

LILA   Hi, Kenny!

KENNY   Lila, I wish you'd take this as a present.

LILA   Kenny!

KENNY   I *want* you to have it, Lila.

LILA   All right, Kenny.

KENNY   And I hope you're going to be very happy, Lila.

LILA   Thanks, Kenny.

KENNY Well . . . so long.

LILA It's awful nice of you to give me the watch, Kenny.

KENNY It's nice of you to take it, Lila.

LILA G'by, Kenny!
(He smiles at her and goes into the living room as LILA *goes into the hallway to the bathroom.* JELLY *comes running into the house unannounced)*

JELLY I bet *I* know why ya din come over last night. I bet *I* know.

KENNY *(His mind elsewhere)* What are ya talkin' about, Jell?

JELLY *(Pointing into* LILA's *room, to a piece of her lingerie on a chair)* You been gettin' that, haven't ya, Ken?

KENNY *(Abstractedly)* Huh?

JELLY Don't try to fool *me*, Ken. You been gettin' that ev'ry night.

KENNY *(Disdainfully)* Why don't you grow up?

JELLY Don't ack so damn superior, Ken. Tell me about it. What'd she do?

KENNY *(With sudden ferocity, grabbing* JELLY's *collar)* If you don't shut up, I'm gonna kill ya.

JELLY Fer cryin' out loud, what ya gettin' so sore about?

120

KENNY   I just don't go for that talk.

JELLY   What's got into you?

KENNY   . . . It's a serious business, making love. I can't kid around about it any more. I . . . I don't want to.

JELLY   Well, gee! I din think I was casting any asparagus on anyone.

KENNY   Forget it, Jelly.

JELLY   Well, do ya want the room, or don't ya?

KENNY   I guess not, Jell.

JELLY   My mom worked hard gettin' the room ready for ya. She put clean sheets on the bed, an' everything.
         (KENNY *takes out his pack of cigarettes*)

KENNY   Here!

JELLY   Oh. Thanks, Ken. You're a pal.
         (JELLY *runs off.* KENNY *stands a moment, weighing his thoughts.* HELEN *returns now, having got herself under control*)

HELEN   You gave *her* the watch, didn't you?

KENNY   Yes.

HELEN   You worked awfully hard for that money. You may need it some day.

KENNY There's times when a man has to give something, Mom.

HELEN Well . . . it was a lovely present.

KENNY Mom . . . I've decided to leave.

HELEN When?

KENNY As soon as they get someone to take my place at the station.

HELEN Where will you go?

KENNY Somewhere. I dunno. Maybe I can still get that job over in Wichita.

HELEN All right, Son. I understand.

KENNY I hate to think of you here alone, but . . .

HELEN Let me deal with loneliness for myself.

KENNY Good-by, Mom.
     (*He embraces her warmly*)

HELEN Good-by . . . (*Now he departs*) . . . Kenneth. (HELEN *goes to* LILA's *room to find her packing*) How do you feel now, Lila?

LILA I'm OK. (*She giggles*) That pill you gave me makes me feel a little light-headed.

HELEN It's phenobarb. It'll wear off after a few hours.

LILA   Yah. It always does.

HELEN   Are you sure you feel like going now, Lila?

LILA   Yes. To tell the truth, I'm gettin' kinda restless. I gotta be goin' somewhere. I guess it doesn't much matter where.

HELEN   (*Picking up a suitcase*)   Here, let me help you. (*Each carrying a suitcase, they go to the front porch.* HELEN *sits,* LILA *remains standing, leaning against a column by the step. She carries her leopard coat over one arm, hiding the bandage. There is a peaceful sadness about her now, her eyes moist with tears. But the morning is beautiful. The sun is out in full now, and the bushes around the house are heavy with roses. School bells ring gladly in the distance.* LILA *surveys the morning scene as though it were her last day of grace upon the earth.* HELEN *looks repentant*) Last night you told me of your sins, Lila, and I regretted them. But you're fortunate in one way. Your sins have always been out in the open where you can see them. Some people hide their sins so deeply in their hearts, they never know they're there.

LILA   Other people? I guess I've always felt no one in the world ever had any sins but me.

HELEN   Other people have lots of sins you never hear about.

LILA   (*Sounding tired*)   Well, I guess we all have to live with our sins as best we can.

HELEN   Lila! how could you have done it?

LILA   I dunno. Mosta the time I do a pretty good job of keeping

123

my spirits up, but there's other times when I feel I just don't wanta live.

HELEN   Lila! Pretty little Lila Green.

LILA   It's been awful nice of you to let me stay, Helen.

HELEN   I was glad to have you, Lila. We'll miss you.

LILA   Thanks.

HELEN   And I hope you'll like the new job.

LILA   (*Embarrassed, figuring the less said the better*)   Oh yah, well . . .

HELEN   And I hope you'll be happy.

LILA   Maybe I *will* be. Who knows?

HELEN   (*Brightening*)   That's the spirit. Might as well look on the bright side. Who knows? You're still young and pretty. You should find a man who really loves you, and . . .

LILA   Oh, I've given up any crazy notions like that, Helen.

HELEN   Don't be pessimistic.

LILA   I've lived my whole life thinking some wonderful man'd fall in love with me some day and marry me. I guess it's all just another one of those childish "illusions" the doctor up in North Dakota warned me about. Maybe I'll be happier now that I don't expect it any more.

(*A young mother comes on now, leading her six-year-old*

daughter by the hand to the child's first day of school. The little girl is dressed in her infant best, all ruffles and ribbons, and she carries a large bouquet of roses. The mother sees HELEN *and speaks*)

MRS. MULVANEY Good morning, Mrs. Baird. My, it's a lovely morning, isn't it?

HELEN Good morning, Mrs. Mulvaney. Are you taking little Sandra to her first day of school?

MRS. MULVANEY Yes. Her first day of school. She's a big girl now, ready to learn her ABC's. Say good morning to Mrs. Baird, Sandra.

SANDRA Good morning, Mrs. Baird.

HELEN Good morning, Sandra.
      (*Mother and daughter walk off now. The school bells ring.* LILA *has watched the scene almost with pain, so envious is she of Sandra's innocence*)

LILA I remember *my* first day of school. Mother took me by the hand and *I* carried a bouquet of roses, too. Mama had let me pick the loveliest roses I could find in the garden, and the teacher thanked me for them. Then Mama left me and I felt kinda scared, 'cause I'd never been any place before without her; but she told me Teacher would be Mama to me at school, and would treat me just as nice as she did. So I took my seat with all the other kids, their faces so strange and new to me. And I started talking with a little boy across the aisle. I din know it was against the rules. But Teacher came back and slapped me, so hard that I cried, and I ran to the door 'cause I wanted to run home to Mama quick as I could. But Teacher grabbed me by the hand and pulled me back to my seat. She said I was too big a girl to be running home to Mama and I had to learn to take my punishment when I broke the rules. But I still cried. I told Teacher I wanted back my roses. But she wouldn't give them to me. She shook her finger and said, when I gave away lovely presents, I couldn't expect to get them back . . . I guess I never learned that lesson very well. There's so many things I still want back.

(*The sound of a car is heard now, pulling up at the side of the house*)

HELEN   I think that's Ricky, Lila.

LILA (*Looking over left*)   Yah. That's him.

HELEN   That looks like a beautiful new car he's driving (RICKY *comes on now*) Good morning, Mr. Powers.

RICKY   G'morning.
(RICKY *picks up* LILA's *suitcases*)

HELEN (*Jokingly*)   I trust you're going to take good care of our girl now.

RICKY   Yah.

LILA (*Embracing her*)   G'by, Helen.

HELEN   Good-by, Lila. Write us sometime. Let us know how you are.

LILA   Sure.
(LILA *walks off the doorstep, joining* RICKY)

RICKY This all ya got?

LILA All my worldly possessions.
(They start off left together, HELEN *watching)*

RICKY *(Out of* HELEN's *hearing range)* Where's the kid? I thought he'd be out here on a white horse to protect ya.

LILA No. No one's gonna proteck me.
(They disappear off left, as HELEN *goes inside the house, closing the door behind her. School bells still ring in the distance)*

Curtain

a
loss
of
roses

by

William Inge

"Inge has probed gently and with sympathy into the characters of these people. Since he writes with skill and clarity, Inge has transferred this sympathy to me." Thus wrote the New York *Daily News* critic, John Chapman, of *A Loss of Roses,* which opened at the Eugene O'Neill Theatre on November 28, 1959. In his foreword to this edition, author William Inge candidly discusses his feelings about the play.

Ever since his *Come Back, Little Sheba* caused the New York Drama Critics' Circle to acclaim him "the most promising new playwright of 1950," William Inge has been regarded as one of the most important American playwrights

(Continued on back flap)

(Continued from front flap)

of the mid-century era.

In 1953 Mr. Inge's *Pic*
Pulitzer Prize, the New
Critics' Circle Award and
Award. In 1955 his *Bus*
even greater success tha
plays, running sixty weel
and then being presented
separate companies. His
way play, *The Dark at*
Stairs, opened to critical
cember, 1957. It was base
initial script, *Farther Off*
which was brought to t
Margo Jones by Tennesse
was produced by Miss
mous Dallas Theatre in

William Inge was bo
ence, Kansas; he was gra
University of Kansas, a
high school in Colum
Stephens College in Colu
and at Washington
St. Louis. He was a radi
Wichita, Kansas, and a
for the St. Louis *Star-Tim*
in New York since his fi
Come Back, Little Sheba.